MW00460725

The Purposes of the University

UNIVERSITY PRESS OF FLORIDA

Florida A&M University, Tallahassee
Florida Atlantic University, Boca Raton
Florida Gulf Coast University, Ft. Myers
Florida International University, Miami
Florida State University, Tallahassee
New College of Florida, Sarasota
University of Central Florida, Orlando
University of Florida, Gainesville
University of North Florida, Jacksonville
University of South Florida, Tampa
University of West Florida, Pensacola

The Purposes
of the University

SELECTED SPEECHES

Bernie Machen

with Aaron Hoover

UNIVERSITY PRESS OF FLORIDA

Gainesville · Tallahassee · Tampa · Boca Raton
Pensacola · Orlando · Miami · Jacksonville · Ft. Myers · Sarasota

Frontis: Photograph © Eric Zamora/UF Photography.

Copyright 2014 by University of Florida Foundation

All rights reserved

Printed in the United States of America on acid-free paper

This book may be available in an electronic edition.

19 18 17 16 15 14   6 5 4 3 2 1

A record of cataloging-in-publication data is available
from the Library of Congress.

ISBN 978-0-8130-6005-7

University Press of Florida
15 Northwest 15th Street
Gainesville, FL 32611-2079
http://www.upf.com

Contents

Preface

Digital technology may have all but killed off newspapers and threatened books, but it has left untouched a far older way of reaching an audience with words: the speech.

We see this in politics, where the stump speech remains a staple, and in the private sector, where the keynote still anchors every conference. In my world of the university, no amount of excitement over the latest smart phone or social media app seems to slow the invitations for me to appear in person, stand before an audience, and speak.

As a result of this tradition, I have given hundreds of speeches in my ten years at the University of Florida, addressing topics weighty, sad, joyous, timely, controversial, and whimsical.

I have discussed my hopes and fears for UF in annual State of the University speeches. I have mourned the loss of students and faculty in eulogies. I have found the higher truth in celebrations of new buildings, spelled out changes in the university's direction, trumpeted the sciences, defended the liberal arts, and pleaded as artfully as possible for donors to prove their generosity.

Like those few Jurassic creatures that flourish today, the speech seems to persist in this iPhone era because it has no need for evolutionary adaptation. Amid an impersonal electronic din, people yearn for the shared intimacy of mutual understanding attainable only between live speaker and live audience.

It is not easy to achieve that intimacy when speaking, and impossible in print. But once the moment of delivery is passed, the speech retains its value as a uniquely contemporary window into the speaker's times. In hopes of preserving that window into UF between 2004 and 2014, I offer the selection of speeches in this book.

Many of these speeches naturally reflect the priorities of my presidency: valuing access for students of all income levels and races, growing the campus, nurturing research and innovation, seeking to garner a greater share of public and private financial support, and shaping a richer undergraduate experience.

Other speeches record some of the melodies of campus life during my time here. I am hopeful I have preserved at least a small sample of our cherished rituals and ceremonies as well as some of the great luminaries and colorful personalities among our faculty and staff, and our student leaders and thinkers.

Taken as a group, these speeches depict a diverse and thriving university very much woven into the fabric of its community and country. Yet as I write this foreword in October 2013 amid the fading colors and cooling temperatures of Florida's brief fall, UF's standing is viewed as facing an existential threat.

It is said that families will no longer accept rising tuition, impoverishing the future of public universities. That as online higher education proliferates, students will desert the classroom buildings and leafy quadrangles that have shaped the college experience for generations. That a U.S. economy no longer capable of guaranteeing good jobs for those with college degrees calls into question our very reason for existence.

Having spent four decades in higher education, I have seen my share of existential threats come and go. Without diminishing the challenges of the day, I am optimistic about UF's future, and that of our nation's land-grant universities.

I believe our country and our campuses will continue to travel a shared path, a belief that is perhaps best argued by the speeches in this book.

"Our Morrill Act Tradition" (page 181) emphasizes the relevance to today's society of the land-grant universities' founding charter of providing a liberal and practical education; contributing to our economy, culture, and society; and ensuring the opportunity of a college education to students of all races and incomes.

"Grow the Little Fish" (page 115) highlights, through the microcosm of UF's own experience, our universities' concerted efforts to transform faculty members' ideas and inventions into goods and services that people want and use—efforts that have helped to build our communities and states.

"Thinking Deeply in a Twitter World" (page 52) makes clear how university research and scholarship are at the core of meaningful and lasting scientific progress and social change.

"Building Bridges, Bridging Differences" (page 127) draws on the development of UF's East Campus to highlight our universities' town-gown role as a constructive, unifying presence in the Gainesville community.

"All That and More: The True Purposes of College" (page 30) shows that in providing pure knowledge, useful skills, and an abundance of extracurricular possibilities, land-grant universities give many of our nation's brightest students a unique opportunity to find their life's direction.

No doubt, the pushback over rising tuition, the rise of online learning, and many other contemporary challenges will put pressure on the foundations of the land-grant universities depicted in these speeches. But I believe this pressure will, in the final analysis, prove more renewing than debilitating.

In my view, online learning need not diminish bricks-and-mortar classes. Rather, it should encourage the reimagining of the traditional lecture format. That is certainly UF's hope amid the debut year of our fledgling statewide undergraduate online university. As "Inventing Our Future" (page 189) makes plain, we expect the "flipped classroom" and other techniques associated with online teaching to freshen and invigorate all classes—both physical and virtual.

Speaking of UF's horizons more generally: I have never felt more strongly about the quality of our students, the productivity of our faculty, and the capabilities of our physical campus. I hope I communicate these feelings throughout the speeches in this book, from my 2011 Convocation speech, "This Is Your Time and Your University" (page 16), to my celebration in 2013 of the UF Data Center, "A New 'Mental Giant'" (page 106).

These speeches are the product of my opinions, perspectives, goals, and dreams. They are also the result of a unique and intimate collaboration with my speechwriter-partner, Aaron Hoover. Aaron usually knows what I want to say, and should say, before I do. His support and skills are essential to my ability to communicate. The words in this book describe me, and they also define Aaron. Ours is a relationship I cherish and appreciate.

Aaron and I are both greatly assisted in my speaking responsibilities by my staff. Beth Boone manages the copious demands on my office with firmness, precision, and grace. Beth and Susan Smith carefully proofread every speech in this book and provided thoughtful and pertinent background materials for all my speaking engagements. Kylie Emerson, Jamal Sowell, and Donna Stricker all contributed to our efforts. Aaron and I also owe a debt to University Historian Carl Van Ness, whose deep knowledge and resourcefulness in searching UF's archives for relevant historical facts, numbers, and quotations have been invaluable.

Finally, I owe whatever success I've achieved as a speaker, leader, and president to my wife, Chris. With her resilience, energy, and warmth, Chris and I have been close partners throughout this journey, and indeed throughout our long marriage.

First Ladies are regarded as wives to powerful husbands, but Chris has always been her own leader, with her own passions and plans. No need to take my word for it: you may read Chris's speeches in Chapter 8, "A First Lady Speaks" (page 139).

As positive as I feel about UF today, I have likewise never experienced a greater sense of optimism on campus. Time will tell, but there's a palpable excitement that the state and university are finally aligned in the goal of creating a public university to equal Florida's size and national prominence. We are making a major investment in hiring accomplished new faculty, shaping a signature undergraduate experience, and growing the online undergraduate initiative.

It is a promising era, but I will leave the final word to my successors and to their speeches!

The Purposes of the University

1

Words for Students

A University without Walls

Remarks at the Writing on the Wall Ceremony, during which students tear down a wall covered in handwritten insults, January 27, 2012

The Plaza of the Americas is surely one of the most open, public places on the University of Florida campus. Anyone can study or socialize here, hold a protest or have a party.

The freedom of the plaza embodies our vision of UF as an open, public university.

No physical walls surround our campus. We strive to eliminate the walls of class, race, and family background in welcoming all students. And our very purpose of higher education can be seen as knocking down the walls of ignorance and prejudice, fear and hatred.

We believe in the University of Florida as a university without walls. But today, we are reminded that some walls still separate us.

From that wall over there—and from the insults written on its blocks—we know that while there may be few visible walls on campus, many remain hidden within society and within people.

Walls made of the hurt and anger of being labeled, stereotyped, or vilified. Walls that confine rather than protect. Walls that can cast long shadows over parts of our lives.

These private, inner walls can be more pernicious than public, outer walls. Sometimes, they cause depression and substance abuse. Sometimes, they hold people back in their careers. Sometimes, they lead to mistreating others. These walls may be out of sight, but too often, they are in control.

Today, we have the rare privilege of seeing these walls clearly, and confronting them directly. I applaud everyone who wrote a hurtful word on one of those blocks. It may seem a small gesture . . . but from small chinks, tall walls crumble.

The time it will take us to tear that wall down will be short, in a ceremony that happens only once a year. As we enjoy that moment, let us affirm its intent every day—within ourselves, our institutions, and our larger culture.

Let us continue this good work until we are as open, free, and absent of walls as this Plaza of the Americas.

Write Your Own Story

Remarks to Palm Beach County's most accomplished graduating seniors at the Scholastic Achievement Foundation of Palm Beach County, April 9, 2013

I have tremendous responsibilities overseeing 50,000 students, 12,500 employees, and a $4.6 billion budget. But there is nothing as rewarding for me as events such as this evening's dinner. Tonight, I am reminded of the ideal at the heart of college: providing the best opportunities for higher learning to the most deserving students in every generation.

The Scholastic Achievement Foundation of Palm Beach County has championed that ideal for thirty five years. For that, I want to thank the Foundation leadership here, as well as the donors behind the scholarships announced tonight.

My favorite part of this event is hearing from the students about their plans for college and their future. I am pleased . . . actually, I'm thrilled . . . that so many of you will attend the University of Florida. Gators of the Class of 2017, welcome! Once you get settled in Gainesville, I hope you'll come to my office so we can meet in person.

Whether you land at UF or another university this fall, there is something I deeply appreciate about this moment in your lives. Up until now, your stories have largely been written by others. For many of you, it has been your parents who have set out your hopes and dreams. But your achievements, ambitions, and worldviews have also been shaped by family members, teachers, coaches, religious leaders, and friends.

I submit to you, the transition you make when you go to college is that, for the first time, you take control of your path. You get to pick your own major, choose your own career, and, eventually, create your own home. At a deeper level, you get to decide your political beliefs, determine your faith, and learn through trial and error how you wish to live your lives. For the first time, in other words, you get to write your own stories.

Generally speaking, I don't like to talk about myself. In fact, I'll be honest. After nearly 10 years as UF's president, I can count on one hand the number of times I've said anything personal in a speech. But because I remember vividly my own steps and missteps from your time in life, I decided to make an exception this evening. I am going to tell you one thing that happened to me when I, like you, was starting my own story.

I promise to be brief. I have one short anecdote and a couple of simple points. Nothing fancy, and there will be no AP test when I'm done.

You may not be aware that I was a dentist before I became a

university president. In fact, I'm still qualified to practice. I think of myself as dentist first, university president second.

My interest in dentistry began when I was in high school. I had an after-school job with my uncle, who was an orthodontist. I liked working with him, and he liked me, and we mapped out my entire life together. That map put me on a path to go to dentistry school and become an orthodontist, just like him. Then, I would return to my home of Webster Groves, Missouri, where I would reach my final destination: joining my uncle as his partner.

As time passed in his office, something dawned on me about my uncle. He was goodhearted, but he liked to be the captain, the leader. Our ship might one day bear both our names, but the writing in my heart would tell the painful truth. I would never work with him. Only for him.

In those days, you could enter dental school after two years in college. When that time came, I made a decision. Even though it meant giving up a guaranteed job in an established practice, I did not choose orthodontics. Instead, I went into pediatric dentistry.

I won't go into everything that happened after that. But while I was pursuing pediatric dentistry, I had the chance to try my hand at teaching. With time, I entered university leadership as the dean of a dentistry college. I landed a position as provost at the University of Michigan, then president of the University of Utah, where I was before I came to Florida.

I might have had a happy life as an orthodontist in Webster Groves. But I stand before you as the president of the University of Florida because of my decision to write my own story. Not a friend's story. Not my parents' story. Not my uncle's story. My story.

Judging from your plans for five years from now printed on tonight's program, I know many of you are well along this road. However, I also got to read the applications most of you submitted for the scholarships whose winners were announced earlier. While I was struck by your accomplishments, I was moved by the hardships so many of you reckon with.

There are students here whose parents have lost their homes and who have been homeless. There are immigrant students who entered school here in Palm Beach speaking almost no English. One student was bullied so ferociously she became seriously ill. Another had to get a job because her mother, the sole wage-earner in a family of four daughters, became sick and could no longer provide for her and her sisters. In fact, more than a few of the seniors here work part-time to help single parents who can't pay the bills.

Your hardships obviously trouble you. But they should not cripple you. Because your achievements and presence here among Palm Beach County's top graduating seniors despite the odds suggests something important. It suggests you have powerful futures ahead of you.

Don't let someone else write your story, and don't let anything keep you from it. Be true to your heart, be strong, and write your own story.

I know your parents or guardians weren't invited to this dinner this evening. Having given you the advice to disregard their plans for you, I'm as happy as you that they're not around!

However, I think they would be glad to hear what I have to say next.

I have no doubt you are aware of the lackluster economy and scarcity of job opportunities for college graduates. No question, there is serious cause for concern. As the president of a university, I worry all the time about how to give our students a leg up. With all that understood, there have always been opportunities for the world's smartest and most ambitious young people—women and men such as yourselves. And as I see it, your opportunities are particularly rich now, in these remarkable times we live in.

That's because interplay between the global economy and technological change are rapidly transforming some of the world's youngest adults into some of its most influential.

Think of Mark Zuckerberg, who was a college sophomore when he created a new global paradigm for social interaction with

Facebook. While Zuckerberg, now 28, may practically be ready for retirement, there are plenty of others eager to follow his lead. From Kevin Systrum of Instagram, to Pete Cashmore of Mashable, to Daniel Elk of Spotify, the Millennial generation is driving the ever more influential social media and much of technological change in general.

Young people are not only deciding how we talk, they're also determining what we talk about. One of today's most popular and controversial television series is HBO's *Girls*. I am sure the fans of *Girls* in this room know that the creator, and the star, is a 26-year-old, Lena Dunham.

Speaking of cultural influences, perhaps you've heard of Kickstarter, the Internet-based fundraising platform that brings together donors with creative causes. Just four years after it was started, Kickstarter has raised more than $500 million for more than 35,000 projects. Headlines announced last year that Kickstarter was within reach of out-funding the National Endowment for the Arts. Not bad for a startup created by three men just barely over 30!

National politics may seem beyond the reach of the youngest adults. But President Obama's reputation as a great orator surely has something to do with his longtime chief speechwriter. His name is Jon Favreau. He was 27 when he penned Obama's first inaugural address.

As you cast off from your homes on your journey through college, don't let your adversities get in your way, and don't let anyone else write your story. Write your own, and know from Lena Dunham, John Favreau, and others that we live in times when you can make your story great.

That brings me to my third and final point before the AP test. Kidding!

While you are about to chart your own course, there's something even more meaningful about to happen in your lives. You are about to get your first chance to chart the course of others.

You will get the chance to shape the lives of the children that come to your lives and the homes you create for them. I urge you to reflect deeply on your own experiences at home, and strive to build your families as you believe families should be.

You will also get the chance to improve your community of Palm Beach County and your state of Florida. Many of you are already moving in this direction with your ambitions to become public school teachers, water engineers, local doctors, and more.

Finally, with your talents and strengths, you can have outsized influence on our nation and our world. Students in this room want to design technology that enables people with disabilities to live normal lives. They want to battle Alzheimer's disease through cutting-edge research. They want to create more helpful and humane robots. I hope you will do all those things. Because as the famous Millennials at the forefront of technology, culture, and politics are proving, we live in times when you can bring positive change to all of humanity—very, very quickly.

As I wrap up, I want to return ever so briefly to that high school student working for his uncle in Webster Groves, Missouri, a half century ago.

I could never have seen it then, but my decision about my direction in college led to an extraordinarily rich life. I found my passion in pediatric dentistry and then in higher education leadership. I met my wife and the love of my life, Chris. Today, we have three grown children and four beautiful grandchildren. As a university president, I have had the exquisite opportunity of helping thousands of young people launch their adulthoods.

I'll be stepping down from the presidency after a year or two. My pathway is closing, just as yours are opening. I'm confident you will live your own extraordinarily rich lives if you keep in mind the short anecdote and the couple of points I've shared this evening.

Write your own story. Find the strength, whatever your hardships, to tell the powerful story within each of you. Write the best stories you can for your families, your communities, and your country. Live the biographies everyone will read.

Great Beginnings at the UF Hall of Fame

Opening remarks for the UF Hall of Fame Reception,
April 3, 2012

There are a lot of halls of fame in the world. There is the Pro Football Hall of Fame, the Automotive Hall of Fame, and the Rock and Roll Hall of Fame. We have the Insurance Hall of Fame . . . the Origami Hall of Fame . . . and here in the Sunshine State, the Florida Citrus Hall of Fame, the U.S. Astronaut Hall of Fame, and, of course . . . the World Golf Hall of Fame.

Whether serious or quirky, all halls of fame owe their origin to Germany, where the first one was built in the 1830s. And most halls of fame have carried on the tradition of recognizing notable people for their contributions to country or cause.

What's exceptional about the University of Florida Hall of Fame is that it honors our students' potential more than their achievement.

Our Hall of Fame was started in 1921, less than two decades after the University of Florida opened its doors in Gainesville. From very close to the beginning, it was clear that induction into the UF Hall of Fame was an indicator of potential for future leadership and acclaim.

The evidence is unmistakable. Over its nine decades, the UF Hall of Fame has welcomed:

. . .

- UF student Fuller Warren, in 1928. Mr. Warren became Florida's 30th governor—a path also followed by at least two other UF Hall of Famers.
- Student George Smathers, in 1936. Stephen C. O'Connell, in 1938. Student Bob Graham, in 1959. A young Dean Cannon, now Speaker of the Florida House, in 1990.
- Ava Parker, chairwoman of the Florida Board of Governors, was inducted into the UF Hall of Fame in 1987.
- Eugene Pettis, soon to become the first black president of the Florida Bar, received Hall of Fame membership in 1981. And,

- Maryanne Downs, last year's Florida Bar president, is a 1988 UF Hall of Famer.

I would tell you about others, but I want to focus instead on the 25 new inductees to the UF Hall of Fame this evening.

Whether seniors or graduate students, they are all impressive. They are Supreme Court clerks, teachers, mentors, entrepreneurs, and scholars. They have served in top leadership positions in student government, led fraternities and sororities, captained athletic teams, and much more.

They have all made lasting contributions to our university and our community.

Inductees, I congratulate you. I hope you will always treasure this honor.

And I also hope that you will follow our proud UF Hall of Fame tradition—and make this the first of many enduring accolades in your lives of leadership and good works.

John Steinbeck, the iPhone, and the Value of a Well-Rounded Life

Remarks at the Cum Laude Society Induction Ceremony, Oak Hall School, February 27, 2007

Recently the *Gainesville Sun* had a story about a teenager who wrote a novel. Perhaps you saw it. Thirteen-year-old Nancy Yi Fan's book will be published by HarperCollins. With that kind of success at this young age, you have to believe Nancy has a remarkably promising future as a writer.

Well, that's how some people find their role in life. Others kind of move along, going from this to that, until they become . . . oh, I don't know, a university president. I earned my doctorate in dental surgery, which has nothing to do with running one of the nation's largest public universities, unless you count the pulling teeth and laughing gas parts.

But exactly how I got here is a story for another day. What I have learned in my life, and what I want to tell you in this speech, is pretty simple: it's good to try many things, and even better to succeed at them.

Let me pause here to say "congratulations" to today's Cum Laude Society inductees. Cum Laude's standards are high, and I know you worked hard. I also want to recognize your parents and families. And I would like to applaud Oak Hall for hosting a Cum Laude chapter.

I like the Cum Laude Society because it rewards students for performing well in all academic subjects. This is also a great thing about high school. In high school, you are forced to cast your net wide. And that can mean pulling in unexpected treasure.

We often hear that success is all about becoming an expert. To be sure, some experts earn a lot of money. But in the big picture, being an expert, if that's *all* you are, is a bad idea for your career and life. By rewarding your talent in many different areas, the Cum Laude Society is giving you a better roadmap for success and happiness.

I understand that Oak Hall has a comprehensive program that includes art. I am told that most high school students here take at least two art classes.

Art. Why art?

Seniors, if you want to strike fear into your parents' hearts, tell them you want to major in art in college.

That may be how the parents of a guy named Chad Hurley reacted when he decided to major in fine arts at Indiana University of Pennsylvania.

After graduating about a decade ago, Hurley made his way to California, where he got a job for a small Internet company. You may have heard of it—PayPal?

There, he tapped his fine arts background to design the PayPal logo, as well as the company's first T-shirts. Hurley stayed at PayPal for a while, then started casting around for other work. After a party with a bunch of friends, he discovered it was impossible to share videos online. The files were too big and took too long to upload. So Hurley founded another little Internet company. Oh, you may have heard of this one, too. It's called YouTube.

YouTube was bought by Google late last year for $1.65 billion. Hurley's share was reported to be more than $300 million, depending on the value of Google's stock. This year, Hurley, the fine arts major from the little-known college, turns 30.

I am not saying that if you major in fine arts you will go on to start the next Internet phenomenon. And I am certainly not saying that you shouldn't pursue art for its own sake. What I am saying is that if you enjoy art, chances are it will be useful to you in ways you never anticipate. Even if you become a stockbroker or a scientist.

Speaking of stockbrokers . . . I gleaned some of the information about Hurley from the phenomenally popular and free online encyclopedia, Wikipedia. I bet your teachers tell you that's not a good idea because Wikipedia can be less than reliable. But that's okay for me because Oak Hall said I would pass today if all I got for this speech was a C!

Anyway, Wikipedia was founded by a fellow named Jimmy Wales, who you may know makes his home just down the road in St. Petersburg. Wales earned his bachelor's and master's degrees not in fine arts, but in finance.

He got wealthy as an options trader in Chicago before starting Wikipedia. Wales loved numbers. But as a child, he also loved encyclopedias.

So let me walk you through this: a child who loves encyclopedias, which are about everything in the world, gets rich in the financial markets. Then he returns to his passion by pioneering a new way of exploring everything in the world. Could there be a better example of the power of being well rounded?

Actually, there is.

There was another youngster who loved encyclopedias so much that when he was eight years old, he read the *World Book Encyclopedia* all the way through the "Ps." That kid was Microsoft founder Bill Gates.

Why he stopped at the "P" I'm not sure. A biography I read said that after "P," he got interested in other activities. Presumably that included "S," for software.

Now just so you don't think I am overly focused on the computer world, let me tell you about a few other successful people and their unlikely roadmaps.

Russell Simmons is the founder of the Phat Farm and Baby Phat clothing lines, and co-founder of Def Jam music. Simmons majored in sociology at City College of New York. In his spare time, he pursued his passion promoting early hip-hop block parties and club shows. Not an academic thing, perhaps, but one that changed Simmons and our culture.

Secretary of State Condoleezza Rice earned her college degree in political science. But as a child, her parents pushed her to study French, music, figure skating, ballet, and other subjects. She remains an accomplished pianist who performs in Washington, D.C., with a chamber music group. I think her parents were onto something.

Bodybuilder, turned Terminator, turned California governor, turned anti–global warming advocate Arnold Schwarzenegger. Enough said.

Okay, so are you starting to see a pattern here? The thread connecting this or that passion in a person's past to their future isn't always obvious. But it is there. Pursuing a wide range of interests is more than a means to an end. It's a style of life, a way to think about thinking. It opens your mind and lets ideas in, and that's what really matters.

As John Steinbeck wrote, "Ideas are like rabbits. You get a couple and learn how to handle them, and pretty soon you have a dozen."

I want to close with one final quick story from the computer world.

Most of you know Steve Jobs as the CEO of Apple Computer, the company behind the iPod and the iPhone. But I am old enough to remember Steve Jobs, the creative genius behind the first Apple Macintosh, which was pretty much the computer that changed everything.

Before the Mac appeared, computers were strange, unwieldy, unapproachable things. You really didn't want to get too close to one. After the Mac, we couldn't get close enough.

Anyway, Steve Jobs gave the commencement address at Stanford a couple of years ago. He told the story of how, while a young man, he took a class in calligraphy at Reed College. He didn't have a plan, and taking that class made no sense. But he liked the way calligraphy looked, and he enjoyed learning about this fine and delicate art.

A decade later, when Jobs was designing the Mac, it occurred to him that computers didn't have to rely on ugly uniform type—type that screamed "I am on a computer!" In fact, computers could have beautiful fonts and gorgeous type.

The Mac embodied that decision. It wasn't just an ugly clunky box unpleasant to lay your hands on. It was nice-looking, fun, and attractive to use. It was an artful machine or, if you like, just plain art. Apple's products still have that reputation today.

To you, Cum Laude Society inductees, and to all the students here, I say keep your minds and your options open. Try many new things, even if they don't seem to have a point. If you do, and I know you will, it will lead to your own YouVisions and iSuccesses.

Reshaping College for the Better

Remarks at Convocation for the inaugural class of the
Innovation Academy, January 4, 2013

Students, you have earned every right to be proud of your achievement and excited about your future at UF. Yet, it's understandable if you feel a few butterflies.

Unlike generations of 18- or 19-year-olds before you, you begin your first semester in the spring rather than the fall. And, out of this year's enrollment of 49,975 traditional students, you are among just 331 brave souls who have elected to participate in this spring-summer Innovation Academy—a new program that is untested on this campus and unprecedented in this country.

I want to assure you that our faculty and staff support the Innovation Academy and are fully committed to making it a success. But, I also know that it's never easy to choose a new and different path. So, let me try to calm down those butterflies by sharing the sentiments of a true authority on new and different paths, the late Steve Jobs.

"It's more fun," Steve Jobs once remarked, "to be a pirate than to join the Navy."

No one doubts that the traditional college experience . . . the "Navy" as Jobs would see it . . . is overdue for radical change. We can see the seeds of this change in the outcry over high student debt, the growth of online education, and new demands for universities to do a better job of preparing students for successful careers.

Old ideas about what defines college are on the way out. Here at UF, you are what Steve Jobs would describe as the "pirates"—the people who will shape the new ideas.

One of those ideas is the spring-summer schedule. If you and your class prove this concept a success, it will encourage other universities to remain open, active, and filled with students for more of the calendar year. Today, because of the limited number of spots for students attending in the spring-fall semesters, many qualified students are turned away from public universities. Tomorrow, because of you, we will admit more students with no sacrifice to our quality.

The academy's emphasis on innovation may also bring welcome and needed change.

Many of the nation's most famous college-age entrepreneurs . . . Steve Jobs, Bill Gates, and Mark Zuckerberg, to name just three . . . only became successful after they dropped out.

Gainesville's innovation community is thriving, with dozens of fast-moving startups headed by UF graduates. This is the right time, and Gainesville is the right place, to turn a new page in this history.

With the Innovation Academy, we have a new opportunity to make sure the next generation of successful technology entrepreneurs are not graduates, and not dropouts, but current college students . . . Innovation Academy students . . . hopefully, many of you!

As I wrap up, I want to note that the Innovation Academy will not be the first new program with the capacity to reshape college for the better. In fact, UF started another new program nearly a century ago that proved to have exactly that influence.

That program was summer school.

Launched 99 years ago this fall, summer school was unique in one very important respect beyond its summer schedule. In 1913, only men were allowed to attend regular college. From the outset, however, UF's summer school program admitted women.

Because of summer school, UF graduated its first woman all the way back in 1920. That was a full 27 years before the university officially became coeducational and began admitting women to its regular fall-spring academic year.

Today, of course, women far outnumber men at the University of Florida and on most college campuses. Equal access and opportunity are foundations of our public universities—and our state and society are much the better for this transformation.

Who knows what antiquated conventions and traditions you,

our Innovation Academy "pirates," will overturn? Who knows what new ideas you will establish . . . or innovate? I, for one, can't wait to find out!

This Is Your Time and Your University

Remarks at Student Convocation, August 19, 2011

Class of 2015, welcome to the University of Florida. We've been waiting for you! And welcome also, mothers, fathers, brothers, sisters, family, and friends. We are thrilled you are here to cheer on your loved ones as they embark on their college careers.

Students, most of you are residents of Florida, and you also arrive from practically every state and dozens of countries.

The journey you begin today makes you part of one of our state's grandest traditions. When you walk to class in the shadow of Century Tower, when your cheers thunder through the stands of Ben Hill Griffin Stadium, you step into the shoes of students who went on to become Florida legislators, governors, and Supreme Court justices; leaders in medicine, business, and engineering; great scientists and noted thinkers.

At the same time, all of you arrive at Florida's flagship university with the global perspective of your generation—and many of you expect careers that may take you beyond Florida, beyond the U.S., to India, China, and elsewhere.

Many previous classes have begun their journeys at UF amid struggling economies and high unemployment. Few have been as compelled as this class to build careers online and internationally.

Like the students before you, you will have to choose your classes wisely and work diligently to prepare for life after college. Unlike them, you will look toward a horizon with fewer boundaries—and with the recognition that your peers in Asia, Europe, and South America are as competitive, driven, and eager to achieve great things as you.

Florida and the world await you. But for the next four years, I urge you to open yourself to all the experiences that this vast university has to offer.

We chose you carefully from 29,269 applicants, and we know that you are already Eagle Scouts, champion sailors, youth symphony directors, Congressional pages, star debaters, and much, much more. It is for *you* to decide whether to continue to build on these achievements or to strike out in new directions.

For the next four years, this is *your* time and *your* university. We will do all we can to inspire you—and we have every faith that you, and the University of Florida, will be better from your time here.

Treat Time as a River

Commencement address to the graduates of Miami Dade College's Kendall Campus, Miami, April 28, 2012

Miami Dade College trustees, faculty, families, friends, and especially, graduates of the Class of 2012 . . . greetings and congratulations! It is an honor to join you here at Kendall Campus, in beautiful Miami, and most of all at Miami Dade College, the largest and most dynamic higher-education institution in the nation.

This is a great day, and I will be thrilled to have my MDC honorary degree and—with all due respect to the Florida Gators—be an MDC Shark. I hear that a few of you will be joining us at UF in the fall. Come by my office at 226 Tigert Hall or email me if I can help a fellow Shark in Gator country. We can't wait to see you!

Graduates, this afternoon, your achievement stands as an out-standing example to your communities; to your siblings and friends; and, for some of you, to your own children. For those graduates who have partners, I want to applaud those partners—for standing by you, and for pitching in more than their fair share so that you could earn your degree just as my wife, Chris, did for me.

To the parents and grandparents here, I applaud you as well. Being a father of three college graduates myself, I share your joy—and your relief! And finally, to MDC faculty, your professionalism and personal attention helped these graduates reach a milestone that will enrich them in ways we cannot even imagine. This moment is what our lives' work is all about.

As you might imagine, I've been part of a few commencement ceremonies in my time. In fact, you won't believe this, but I gave my first commencement address fifty years ago this summer, as a senior in high school in Missouri. It's true. Chris still keeps an old copy of my speech around to torture me.

I devoted part of that speech to astronaut John Glenn, who in that year of 1962 had become the first American to orbit the world. He launched from here in Florida aboard a Mercury space capsule called *Friendship 7*. We were in the midst of the Cold War, and Glenn's flight brought great relief that the U.S. could compete with the Soviet Union.

But his historic trip did something that has far outlasted the rivalry between our superpowers: it connected the U.S. with friendly nations in a way we had never been connected before. That bond was brought home by Glenn's flight over Australia, where residents of the city of Perth turned on their lights in a glowing "hello" to the American astronaut passing by in the dark loneliness of space.

I have no doubt that, this weekend, other commencement speakers at other campuses around the nation are telling graduates that if they want to succeed, they have to learn to connect with other parts of the world—just the way Astronaut Glenn did five decades ago. They are advising that we live in a global economy now, one that requires professionals to work in different countries, speak multiple languages, and thrive in cultures foreign to their own.

That wisdom of the world, which we strive to instill in all college students, *already dwells within each of you.*

You live in Miami, one of the nation's most multicultural cities. You gather from more than 58 different countries at MDC, a richly diverse university that graduates the highest numbers of minorities of any college. Four out of five of you trace your roots to Cuba or Latin America.

Those origins place you among the nation's fastest-growing minority population of more than 50 million Hispanics—in an America where, in about 35 years, minorities will become the majority.

You are among a privileged group of new college graduates who know our country and world as they are becoming. *You won't have to catch up to the times. The times have to catch up to you.*

As Miamians and MDC graduates entering a world of fewer national barriers, your multiculturalism equips you to form strong bonds across countries and cultures. This ability will accelerate your careers and increase your incomes, and it will also boost the world's global stability, from economics to human rights.

But while your cultural and language fluencies will help you do good as you do well, they will not be enough. Especially in our divided times, it will be crucial for you to look deeply within yourselves to bring *compassion* and *acceptance* to all your ventures.

I'll tell you another story. I was the oldest child in a middle-class family of five in a suburb of St. Louis. Like many of your parents, my parents believed if I wanted something, I should work for it. I started doing odd jobs when I was eight years old, and by high school, I needed my first real job.

It was just before Christmas, and our town's department store, Lambert's, was hiring. There was only one hitch: everyone was terrified of the owner, who chased teenagers out of his store and was widely reviled as the meanest businessman in town. Nevertheless, my mother, a schoolteacher, told me to ask him for a job. I did not want to do it—I was scared. But she insisted. So I mustered all my courage and walked through the doors alone.

My first surprise was that I got the job. My second was that as my hours piled up in the store, I grew to like and respect this man and he to like and respect me.

Before long, I left Lambert's and headed off to college. But the experience taught me a lesson that has endured for my whole life: never rely on the opinions of others. I try to begin relationships with openness, and to form *my own judgments* of people.

I believe that lesson is at the heart of my career, which has followed an unusual path. Although I trained as a dentist, earning both a doctor of dental surgery and a master of science in pediatric dentistry, I found my calling in higher-education leadership. I am the only dentist who is a major university president.

It wasn't my technical education or dental skills that got me here. I wasn't born into this role, and no one gave me any special favors. I oversee a $5 billion budget without an accounting degree; a major sports conglomerate with no background in sports management; and a huge university health science center with no recent experience in health care. But I do know something of dealing with people. And my leadership responsibilities require managing 12,000 of them, in every race, religion, nationality, and personality type.

In your personal interactions, do not be a *fortress*, steeled against people. Be a *forest*, serene and open to them finding a path to your heart.

I began this afternoon talking to you about John Glenn and *space*. I want to end by telling you something about *time*.

When I was in college in the wake of John Glenn, everyone recognized space as the new frontier. Today—with the shuttle Discovery's installation at the Smithsonian bringing a symbolic end to the space age—there is less consensus about where the greatest promise lies for you. Some say it is globalization. Others, innovation. But I would like to suggest that one of your great frontiers is *time*.

Everything in your world insists that time is instantaneous.

Tweeting, texting, Facebook: all give you and your smart phone so much information, so quickly, they seem to *collapse* time, leaving you with scarcely any time to respond before the next burst of incoming information.

And technology is only part of the urgency of 2012. Politics and fads . . . success and fame . . . human relationships . . . all seem to flare and fade in an instant. Or perhaps I should say, "Instagram." That is the photo-sharing company Facebook just purchased for a billion dollars. It was formed by a dozen twenty-somethings *less than two years ago*.

From Instagram to the iPhone, today's sense of urgency has generated a great deal of financial success. This wealth may or may not be real, as recent booms and busts teach us. Either way, I believe it has come at a cost. That cost is the sense of *hyper-alertness*, just short of frantic, that prevails throughout our society.

People are not learning much from the past these days. As a matter of fact, they aren't really fixated on what's happening in the here-and-now, or what awaits down the road. Instead, they exist in that strange moment that accompanies the incoming text or news flash—the moment just beyond the present but never far enough ahead to call the future. They're *seizing every instant* and *losing every day*.

As the graduates of 2012, your generation is destined to live longer than any generation in history. I want to assure you that you have time. And I want to suggest that *your frontier* is to recapture and revive your time. Because time is truly *a gift*.

So, my take-home message is: Slow down! Breathe! Be in the present! Think about today! Today! Find the time to ask yourselves . . . what's the hurry? Consider the moment. Open yourself to unscheduled possibilities.

Take the class outside your major—it may speak to your soul. Meet the person not planned into your day—she or he may become your life's partner. Visit a new city on a whim—you may decide to make it your home.

Treat time not as a *race* but as a *river*, bearing you slowly and gently into the wide gulf of adventures and experiences that map who you are.

The author William Faulkner wrote, "Only when the clock stops does time come to life." His point was that life is most complete when you give yourself the luxury to embrace it in all its richness. Not just work and weekends. Not just personal passions and travel. But also, friends, families, and children—all enjoyed with leisure and appreciation.

As MDC graduates, you are already light years ahead of your contemporaries in the cross-cultural proficiency that—just like John Glenn—will make you friends and bring you success wherever your careers take you. But do not forget that you also have *an ocean* of time.

So, have the longer-than-text conversation. Read the thicker book. Take the extended vacation. Linger with family. Lengthen all of life's celebrations. Especially the one this afternoon—you deserve it.

UF Student Government on Its Centennial

Remarks at the Centennial Celebration of UF Student Government, Student Government General Assembly, November 17, 2009

Student government has a long history at the University of Florida. But, let me say this: UF is in a new era. Student government has never been as important as it is today. It is also the most powerful I have seen.

You may trace your origins to 1909. But, as UF confronts the realities of 2009, student government matters more than ever.

We need students to get behind improvements here at UF. We also need an active, passionate student voice in moving UF forward statewide and nationally. Your history proves you can do both.

Thanks to you, in decades past, students paid for Lake Wauburg and chipped in for the O'Connell Center. Student fees supported the Marston Science Library, Criser Hall, the Student Health Care Center, the South End Zone, and Baby Gator Child Care.

The bus system is a tremendous success only because of financial support from student fees.

With your leadership, students paid for our student recreation centers. You built the original Reitz Union and paid for the renovations. You are now a champion of our next big improvement in student facilities—the quote-unquote "new" Reitz.

Over the past couple of years we headed up a campaign to win the right to raise tuition to the national average. We threw everything we had at this campaign—lobbying lawmakers, wooing newspaper editorial boards, making our case in civic clubs.

But you know what our linchpin was? Student support. We never would have been successful without you and your advocacy.

This is not an aberration, not in this new era. It is clear to me, student government is uniquely poised to help UF meet the challenges ahead.

With control of a $14-million-plus budget, you have always been powerful. But that power increased eight years ago, when Florida adopted the Boards of Trustees system, giving student government presidents equal votes on universities' top governing boards.

You have illustrious alumni. People who have made great contributions to Florida, such as the late Stephen C. O'Connell, George Smathers, and Lawton Chiles, Bob Graham, and Reubin Askew.

But also current power brokers. Debbie Wasserman Schultz, Adam Putnam, Dean Cannon, Marshall Criser, Steve Uhlfelder, and Danny Ponce. Many others—and many prominent people in the private sector too.

With so much at stake for this university, your bond with these influential personalities matters in 2009 more than ever.

This fall's news that enrollment at the University of Central Florida had eclipsed enrollment at UF was no concern to us, as we have been whittling away at our undergraduate numbers for some time. Nevertheless, it signaled a major shift to alumni, and to the state.

UF not the biggest university in Florida? Even a decade ago, it would have been unthinkable. Your voice in positioning this university, not just as a big state school, but also as a top national research institution is absolutely essential.

I understand you are independent. You rightly reflect student concerns and opinions, and sometimes those concerns and opinions run counter to our agenda. We value you tremendously as partners, but we also believe that disagreements can be healthy and good—as long as we never allow them to overwhelm the love we share for the University of Florida.

This is your university. And, with students at the core of UF, we need your ideas, your advocacy and your voices. More than ever, in 2009, 2010, 2011 and for all the years ahead.

At the End of Your Journey, Come Home

Commencement speech delivered at Zhengzhou University,
Zhengzhou, China, June 25, 2010

恭喜所有的毕业生!

Gong-she / da jah / be-yeah-lah! [Congratulations to all the graduates!]

I am grateful today to receive an honorary doctoral degree from Zhengzhou University. And, I am delighted to be a part of this ceremony and to be your commencement speaker.

I want to offer my hearty thanks to President Changyu Shen and his leadership team for inviting and honoring me. President Shen and many others here in Zhengzhou and at Zhengzhou University have made this visit one of the most memorable in my four decades in higher education.

My visits to this campus, and my conversations with professors and students, have made abundantly clear why this university is the best in Henan Province, and one of China's top-ranked "211" universities.

I am proud that my university, the University of Florida, is establishing a special bond with Zhengzhou University.

It is especially interesting for me to visit ZZU because it sheds light on how this country's universities produce the students who pursue advanced degrees at U.S. universities, including the University of Florida.

Last year, American universities hosted 98,510 students from China—803 at the University of Florida, which we call UF.

It is no exaggeration to say that Chinese graduate students compose the backbone of many of the most rigorous engineering and physical science programs at our universities.

I will look forward to sharing with our professors what I learn about how these students get their skills.

I know that some of you will travel to other parts of the world this summer to further your studies. I hope we will see you at UF, one of America's top five largest public universities, with about 50,000 students, 200 degree programs, and an 800-hectare campus.

I would love to welcome you to Gainesville—smaller than Zhengzhou, subtropical, and equidistant in the middle of Florida between the Atlantic ocean and the Gulf of Mexico. In other words, about two hours from the beach and Disney World!

But, whether you plan to study abroad, pursue graduate school in China, or enter the workforce, what I want to tell you today is the same thing I would tell UF graduates.

Zhengzhou and Gainesville may be separated by 12,669 kilometers, a language barrier, and a cultural divide, but graduates from both universities are entering a world more open than ever before.

I would tell UF graduates, and I say to you: Consider all that there is in the world, and try to work internationally. The world—and America—need the unique insight you can bring from China.

And, when you have shared your talents and learned what you can abroad, I urge you to use your experience to benefit Zhengzhou and Henan Province.

China today is not only a world economic leader, but also a standard bearer in many other areas vital to this planet. As the country's newest graduates, you can be ambassadors for China's progressivism.

This is true of renewable energy. China today makes more wind turbines and solar panels than any other nation. From smart electric grids to solar hot water heaters, China dominates. The U.S. and other countries need to follow your aggressive push toward greener energy.

Or, think of transportation. The Chinese government this month announced huge tax breaks for buyers of hybrid and electric vehicles.

Already the world's largest auto market, China will be the world's largest electric car market as early as next year. In China, already number one in high-speed rail, gas stations may soon be antiquities.

The Chinese government is building *charging* stations in five major cities here. Americans are still waiting for this sort of thing!

You may not have studied energy or transportation. But in working abroad, or with international companies or agencies, you can spread forward-thinking perspective on these and other issues vital to our shared future. The 2008 Beijing Olympic motto still stands: "One World, One Dream."

From a purely self-interested standpoint, I hope that your future touches the United States, because you can add new dimensions to a relationship that grows richer by the hour.

U.S. universities continue their traditional role of hosting Chinese students—indeed, the influx of students was up 21 percent last year, driven by an influx of Chinese *undergraduates*.

But, we are also sending more American students here to China. Numbers have been rising steadily, and late last year Presidents Obama and Hu Jintao announced a joint initiative to bring 100,000 Americans to China to study at Chinese universities.

For Chinese graduates, many more doors are opening.

Some Chinese graduate students still elect to stay in the U.S., but more and more return home, to work at Chinese companies. They are now being joined by American college graduates.

A *New York Times* reporter last year found young Americans working at a social media company in Beijing and a law firm in Shanghai. And you know what? It's not just young Americans.

This spring, the chief technology officer of the California firm Applied Materials became the first chief technology officer of a major American technology corporation to move to China.

To be sure, our countries' relationship can be competitive, and our politics and cultures can clash.

But the seeds of competition are also those of cooperation, the notes of disagreement the same as those of harmony.

I, and other Americans, feel a lot of warmth here in China. And, if you were to visit the U.S. today—perhaps I should say *when*—you would find a country keen to learn more about China.

Chinese-language schools are springing up all over—in fact, we now help train teachers of Chinese at UF. In April, when Gainesville hosted the fifth annual Florida Statewide Chinese Competition, attendance almost doubled from the previous year!

Our state tourism officials launched a campaign this spring to lure more Chinese tourists to Florida.

We are completing a major new addition to UF's art museum—specifically for Asian art.

You might be surprised to learn that China is Florida's largest non-Latin trading partner. China-Miami trade alone totaled $393 billion last year.

By choosing to work in the international arena, or by bringing your skills to the U.S., you can help shape this evolving relationship to both our benefit.

We urge you to bring your talents to us, but we also want to come to you, here in China. That is why the University of Florida is among many U.S. universities today who oversee centers in China.

We work with Chinese and American students through our Beijing Center for International Studies. We also promote research collaboration and joint technology development.

UF and ZZU researchers are gearing up for joint research on Parkinson's disease. We plan a collaborative program on hospital management. At least three UF faculty members have taught courses at ZZU.

When you consider how much we have to share, the result of this sort of collaboration will benefit all of us.

Which brings me to my final point.

China and the U.S. share immense challenges. We are both running out of clean water at the very time we must set aside more water to protect nature.

We both face air, water, and industrial pollution problems at a time of increasing understanding of the devastating effects on our health.

Much is reported about the smog in Beijing, but the oil gusher in the Gulf of Mexico is ample evidence that the U.S. has major shortcomings in this area as well.

Poverty, cancer, threats to food production—these are global problems, and the solutions will originate in different parts of the globe.

And, yet, here in Zhengzhou and in Henan Province, you also have your own local challenges, just as we do in Gainesville and Florida.

For our part, we are struggling to diversify our economy and grow our technology industry. We want to balance urbanization with environmental protection. We need to improve secondary schools and Florida's universities.

Most University of Florida graduates eventually settle in Florida. When they do, we hope a global perspective will give them energy and fresh ideas. The same goes for ZZU graduates who return to Zhengzhou or Henan Province.

So, engage with the world, but at some point, bring all that you learn back here, to your beautiful home. You, the world, Henan Province, and Zhengzhou will all be the better for it.

2

The Nature of Education

All That and More:
The True Purposes of College

Common lecture for "The Good Life" course,
January 24, 2013

Thank you, Professor Wolpert, and thank you for inviting me to give the Common Lecture for this one-of-a-kind course. It is my honor to do so. I am especially pleased to have an opportunity to speak to these young women and men so early in their journey at the University of Florida.

Like all the best journeys, the journey through college can be a destination all its own. I hope my remarks this evening will help you make it so.

I hope, too, that you will have questions for me after the lecture. You see, this course is very much about questions. It is the only course I know of whose title takes the form of a question. And, ultimately, finding the Good Life involves questioning. Questioning assumptions. Questioning oneself . . . even questioning a university president!

We're only a couple of weeks into the new semester, so you haven't been in this class long enough to answer the question asked in the title. You may not be sure what the Good Life is. But I bet you've already figured out what it is not.

Let's see . . . watching the bus pass you when you have a 7:25 A.M. exam. Not the Good Life. Getting pulled over by UPD . . . on your bicycle. Not the Good Life. Receiving more texts from the UF Alert system than from your friends. Definitely not the Good Life.

Some of you probably are excited to be in this course. Others may be wondering why you are here . . . and looking for someone to blame. I hope we don't get off to a rocky start if I admit that person would be me.

I began my tenure as UF president nearly 10 years ago. As time passed, I noticed that the university was like a large city. Diverse. Full of energy. But everyone living in their own little worlds. The one event that brought students together occurred only on certain fall Saturdays.

I love Gator home games as much as anyone. But with 50,000 students from more than 200 countries studying on this idyllic campus, I wished and hoped the students could have more in common than cheering together in a stadium. I wanted them to gather around the playing field of ideas.

"What Is the Good Life?" is the university's endeavor to foster the common experience of intellectual questioning—the shared life of discovery.

That was how and why the class originated. But "What Is the Good Life?" has become even more relevant amid the increasing discourse about whether universities should do more to train students for jobs. We hear this concern nationally and in Florida. Here, the public—in particular the governor—is asking whether we do enough to prepare our students for the job market.

That question is appropriate in light of the tough road facing college graduates. The Associated Press reported recently that 53 percent of recent graduates are jobless or underemployed. Fifty-three percent. All you have to do to appreciate the enormity of that number is think about half of you moving back in with your parents after you graduate. Not the Good Life!

Even if the economy bears some blame, universities are negligent if they don't accept more responsibility here. UF has one of the nation's top-ranked career services centers. We are the leading choice for corporate recruiters. Still, we must do more. As a first step, we are surveying graduates to get a clear idea of their success in finding positions—something we should have been doing all along.

This reassessment and improvement of the college-career connection is clearly needed. But that realization begs another important question: Is job placement all that college is for? What is the purpose of college? Does college have a singular purpose or are there multiple purposes?

Let's think about this objectively and go back to the beginning of higher education in Florida. Why has this state invested millions—even billions—of dollars in building the University of Florida?

UF is a land-grant institution. Abraham Lincoln created these kinds of institutions 150 years ago. And, from what I have read about it, the purposes of land-grant institutions were to advance training and research in agriculture, engineering, and the sciences. Preparing students for careers, if you will. And, these institutions were to steep students in the deepest considerations of morality, philosophy, and ethics. Does that sound familiar? Isn't it what "What Is the Good Life?" about?

After my time at UF and six years as president of the University of Utah, I believe that college has many true purposes. Today, I'd like to focus on the question most relevant to you—"What Is the Good Life in College?"—with a discussion of the three purposes I view as most important for you to address while you are here.

First, I am convinced that your time in college remains the single-best opportunity for you to explore who you are and your purpose in life. Second, college is the best place to begin your career. In these tough times, I can't emphasize career enough. Part of your job in college is to graduate with the ability to get a job. Third, college is the best time for you to think beyond your own lives and careers to contributing to the larger world.

Self-discovery. Career. And making a contribution. I propose that if you achieve these three purposes, you will find the Good Life in College.

One way to walk you through each purpose would be to show you how college shaped the lives of famous people.

I figure many of you saw *The Hobbit*. You might be interested to know, it was taking Finnish at Oxford that led J.R.R. Tolkien to become fascinated with languages, including creating his own. That sparked the magical worlds that have fascinated generations of readers. Now that's self-discovery!

Or, I could tell you about Kevin Systrom, the 26-year-old who enrolled in a nine-month entrepreneurship program as an undergraduate at Stanford and went on to start a little company called Instagram. Considering he and his cofounders sold Instagram to Facebook for $1 billion, that Stanford entrepreneurship program was a great career move by an undergraduate!

And, about contributing to the world: think of Rachel Carson, author of *Silent Spring*, the book that launched the modern environmental movement and celebrated its 50th anniversary in 2012. Carson changed her major from English to biology all because of one professor at Pennsylvania College for Women. It was the college major change that has changed the world.

But, as I reflected on the matter, I realized I didn't want to leave you with the impression that finding the Good Life in College is the purview of a Tolkien, a Systrom, or a Carson.

I felt it would be more meaningful to ground my reflections in the experiences of three current UF undergraduates who are just slightly ahead of you on this journey. Far from famous, these students aren't even finished! But, I believe the experience of each embodies one of the three purposes I just outlined—self-discovery, career, and contributing to the world.

I'll begin with a sophomore named Nazeeh Tarsha and his story of self-discovery.

Nazeeh went to Coral Reef Senior High School in Miami, where he was in the academically challenging IB program. Anyone else here from Miami? Too bad we're not gathered at Miami Beach. Now that would be the Good Life!

Nazeeh excelled in math and science at Coral Reef. He earned a high score on the math portion of the SAT. He hung out with other math and science students.

His parents are immigrants. He is the first in his family to go to college. Everyone expected him to pursue a high-paying career in a technical field like computer programming, and he began UF as an engineering major.

Then, in the spring of his freshman year, Nazeeh took an elective called theatre appreciation. He liked it so much, he took two summer electives in improvisation and acting. Suddenly, he was hooked. In fact, he found himself devoting his spare time to reading unassigned plays, just for the sheer pleasure of it.

This past fall, Nazeeh faced a critical choice: continue in the path he and his parents always predicted, or make a radical turn. On September 15, Nazeeh auditioned as an acting major. Three weeks later, he checked his email at 4 A.M. and found out he was accepted. It was all he could do to stop himself from shaking his roommates awake to give them his news!

I did not tell Nazeeh's story to urge you to follow his footsteps into acting. Nor can I claim that Nazeeh's choice will lead to fame or financial bounty.

Although . . . for the record . . . UF counts among its former students actress Faye Dunaway, the band members in Sister Hazel, and the movie director Jonathan Demme.

Demme is best known for directing *The Silence of the Lambs* and

Philadelphia. He came to UF hoping to be a veterinarian and then couldn't pass chemistry. But that's a story for another speech!

I told you Nazeeh's story because he made a couple of decisions I hope you will repeat. One, he took classes that had nothing to do with his background or major. Two, he paid attention when those classes told him something profound about himself.

The poet Robert Frost once said, "College is a refuge from hasty judgment." I hope you will follow Nazeeh's example, and think of Frost's words, as you continue your journey.

Okay. I think we can agree that if you enjoy what you do, you are more likely to be a success. So, those of you who experience self-discovery in college are already a step toward the second true purpose of college, finding a career.

Even if you now have no idea what career you want to pursue, there is much you can do beginning now to pave the way for your first job. Much you can do to minimize the chance that you will move back in with your parents!

It starts with getting informed. With your options still wide open, you owe it to yourselves to learn which bachelor's degrees lead to the best job opportunities and the most pay.

The facts are pretty clear. Here in the Sunshine State, demand for graduates with degrees in science, technology, engineering, and math—the so-called STEM fields—is soaring.

In fact, the state of Florida has estimated that Florida will need 120,000 new professionals in these fields by 2018. STEM job openings increased 14 percent last year over the previous year, to more than 65,000 positions. And this in a slow economy!

STEM occupations include nursing, web development, accounting, systems engineering, and financial analysis. Not only do these fields have the most open positions, they also tend to pay more.

The Chronicle of Higher Education reported this month that nationwide, bachelor's-degree recipients from the class of 2012 who majored in engineering or computer science earned average starting salaries topping $60,000. Those who received degrees in the humanities and social sciences brought home less than $37,000.

This information matters if salary is your goal. But even if it's not, it will help you to get informed about what lies ahead. And not just informed, but also prepared.

Because of the rapidly changing global economy, jobs that are in high demand today may be less valued tomorrow. In your own lifetimes, advances in technology have transformed careers in journalism, which used to deliver the news on something called newsprint. Technology has also transformed the music industry, which once controlled the distribution of popular music; and finance, where stock trading was once done by human beings who earned commissions and is now done mostly online.

This rapid change means you not only need to think about jobs, you also need to think about skills. What skills can you develop that will help you get a job, whatever field you choose?

That question brings me to my next UF student, a Miami resident and senior named Melissa Eizagaechevarria.

An accomplished pianist in high school, Melissa began at UF as a music major who expected to transition to pre-med and head off to medical school.

Music at UF, however, required hours of solitary practicing, and biology entailed lots of memorization. Melissa disliked both practicing and memorization. By contrast, she found she excelled at the on-the-fly problem solving demanded by her physics with calculus class.

Melissa began her junior year without a clear idea of her future. But when a Thanksgiving trip to the National Air and Space Museum proved inspirational, she decided to try aerospace and mechanical engineering. Luckily, that decision proved exactly right.

Like physics with calculus, aerospace and mechanical engineering classes put a premium not on memorizing facts, but on conceptualizing and solving problems. What's more, engineering relies on teamwork, a skill that feels natural to Melissa. Rather than spending hours alone with her piano or a biology textbook, she stays up all night solving problems with her friends on the whiteboards in their apartments.

Today, Melissa has summer internship possibilities at Boeing, Pratt & Whitney, and Honeywell, and she's confident of her professional future.

The take-home message is this: discovering and developing your skills in college—for Melissa, problem-solving and teamwork—may be just the way to identify the career options that will work for you. If you are looking for a career, start by looking at yourself.

Recruiters for companies prefer new employees with the skills of critical thinking, writing, problem-solving, and teamwork.

The "Job Outlook 2013" survey by the National Association of Colleges and Employers found that the top two skills valued by employers are communication and teamwork.

Whether it is a profession like medicine, teaching, or engineering, or a field like business, real estate, or construction, you need to match your interests and abilities with the skills required for success. It's all part of the journey.

So, get informed about where the jobs are. And use these four years to discover and hone your skills.

Ultimately, preparing for your career is about so much more than jobs and income. As the educator and author Peter Drucker wrote, "Work is an extension of personality. It is achievement. It is one of the ways in which a person measures his or her worth and humanity."

So far, I have devoted my thoughts to how students can make the most of the college experience for themselves. First, the process of self-discovery. Next, steps to career.

Now, I would like to turn to that third true purpose of college: contributing to the larger world.

David Foster Wallace, the late author of the acclaimed 1996 novel *Infinite Jest*, captured the essence of this idea. He said that college is a place where you can learn, quote, "to be aware that there are other realities outside yourself—so you don't walk around in a bubble of certainty that your universe is the only one."

With that thought in mind, let me turn to the third student I want to tell you about today, a senior named Stuart Block from right here in Gainesville.

Stuart's dad and brother were college football players, and he played tennis in high school. He started UF as a sports management major with hopes of becoming a sports agent à la Tom Cruise as Jerry Maguire—or perhaps entering a career in business.

Then, in the fall of his sophomore year, Stuart took a class in sustainability. He was captivated by renewable energy and its promise of clean energy and reducing carbon emissions.

It wasn't long before he changed his major to one newly created at UF: "sustainability in the built environment." By junior year, he was supplementing classes with his own extracurricular project: installing solar cells on the roof of his fraternity, Beta Theta Pi.

Today, the outcome of Stuart's project is a 10-kilowatt, $44,000 system that is only the second solar installment on a fraternity in this country. With just one semester before he graduates, Stuart made his fraternity more environmentally sustainable and built his résumé toward a business career with a focus on energy.

Too often, we are told that we have two choices for life's direction—personal success or sacrifice for a greater cause. As Stuart's experience shows, this is a false dichotomy. We can shape lives that combine personal ambition and social good.

As the late Katherine Graham said, "To love what you do and feel that it matters—how could anything be more fun?"

I think Stuart is well on his way to that happy balance. So, too, are Nazeeh and Melissa. Whether they will remain in their paths I can't say—their journeys continue. But, to me, they have each used their time wisely to find the Good Life in College.

I began this evening with the value of questions—the question in the title of this course, the questions to pose about yourself, your career, and the world beyond.

Stuart, Nazeeh, and Melissa were not afraid to question themselves or their initial ideas of what they would do while at UF. As you discover your life's direction, find a career and learn to pursue the greater good, I hope that you, too, will keep asking questions.

Bricks and Mortar in a Digital Age

Opening remarks for the Bricks and Mortar in a Digital Age Conference at University Auditorium, April 11, 2013

I want to start us off today by asking you to look up at the ceiling. Go ahead, look. If you check the trusses on the sides, you'll see the gargoyles. Are you with me? Look closely and you'll notice there are four different versions, each holding a football, a lyre, a book, and a gear.

Now, look really, really closely. You can tell the figures were made nearly 100 years ago . . . because none of them are checking their phones!

When the University Auditorium was built in 1927, these figures were meant to embody the life of the university—athletics, the arts, scholarship, and science and engineering. In the early days, the entire student body could fit in this one space. We expanded as the population grew, but the auditorium remained the place for commencements, student dramatic productions, and guest speakers.

In the 1950s, people came here to listen to Robert Frost, who wintered in Gainesville and gave annual poetry readings. Later, they filled the seats to see Art Buchwald, Gerald Ford, Betty Shabazz, and Andy Warhol. They gathered for the strength and solace of memorial services after Pearl Harbor, the assassination of President Kennedy . . . and, as many people here will remember, to be reassured by the words of UF's eminent historian Michael Gannon after 9/11.

Today's symposium culminates our yearlong celebration of the 150th anniversary of the Morrill Act that created our nation's land-grant universities. The history of this auditorium captures the good that flowed from that law.

It captures how the Morrill Act expanded university education from the elite to the public. How the act broadened education to embrace liberal arts, agriculture, and science and engineering. How it nurtured research that helped a young country grow and prosper. And, how public land-grant universities became a center of intellectual, cultural, artistic life in our country.

As we come together today, however, there is a deepening sense that the ground is shifting beneath these foundations.

State budget cuts have weakened public universities from Florida to Texas to California. Student debt has reached an all-time high and the public has had it with tuition increases. Competition from for-profit universities gets fiercer and fiercer, and virtual higher education is becoming a viable alternative. A growing chorus is questioning whether traditional college degrees are needed at all.

We must ask, have we reached the end of an era? Are we moving past the time when places like this auditorium are vital to universities, and when universities like the University of Florida are vital to our country?

That is the central theme of today's symposium. And I am looking forward to the dialogue and discussion.

For me, personally, I come today with several tentative hypotheses: I am optimistic about our future. I think Americans will continue to support quality traditional public universities, though perhaps with less blind faith and more questions—a healthy skepticism that will strengthen us.

I believe online education will increase choices for students but not put an end to real classrooms and real campuses. If anything, the online world will prompt bricks-and-mortar universities such as UF to get better at what we do: to make classes more personal and meaningful and campuses even richer places to study and live.

I think the science and scholarship that is our founding charter will continue to be both an economic benefit and public good for our country—and that our government and industry will remain supportive in spite of the expense.

But it's not up to me. And these hypotheses can be challenged. The future of land-grant universities is in the hands of the faculty, staff, political leaders, community members, and students who are here today. You will decide the next step in our journey—and, in the best tradition of public universities, this decision will rest on informed, reasoned, and honest discussion.

So, as we begin our symposium today, I hope you will remember our legacy, take stock of our challenges, and be open to the possibilities of the future. I urge you to hold nothing back and to put your best ideas on the table . . . for in the words of Robert Frost, who once read so many of his poems on this stage, "Freedom lies in being bold."

In Celebration of a New Recreation Center

Remarks at the grand opening of the Southwest Recreation Center, August 24, 2010

This building is stunning! The only shame is you have to exercise here.

I tend to feel like Mark Twain, who is said to have remarked, "Every time I feel the urge to exercise, I sit down until it goes away."

However, I do think Mr. Twain would appreciate the two new massage rooms!

I am sure I am not alone in dreading my workout . . . or in experiencing that euphoric calm that comes after I push myself physically. Exercise is about the health of the body AND the health of the mind. And if you have ever run outside at dawn or swum laps as the sun sets over your shoulder, you know that both are bound up with the health of the planet.

That triad—mind, body, planet—is at the heart of this expansion.

We are just across the street from the UF Cultural Plaza. You can fill your mind at the Natural History Museum or the Harn, nurture your spirit at the Performing Arts Center . . . and take care of your body here.

With its sweeping glass façade, this building feels like the cornerstone for this unique part of campus. And like all great buildings, this one reflects the tenets of our times, ever more attuned to the deep connections between mental and physical well-being.

We are also more and more aware of the connections between nature and health. This building honors those connections. It is UF's first to harvest rainwater for irrigation. What's more, we don't hide the system, shunting the water to an invisible reservoir. No, it is there for all to see outside the front doors, where it is integrated with the public art installation.

Rainwater flows down from the roof and gushes into the large urns by the walls. From the urns it flows through the rock pathways, then into the swales by the sidewalks. There, it nurtures 7,000 native plants.

When you arrived, you may have noted the large columns fronting the entrance, the main element of artist David Dahlquist's piece. He says, and I quote, "the sculptural columns suggest a root structure, *almost like human tissue*, symbolic of the common denominators between plant and animal and our shared dependence on water."

This threading together of mind, body, and nature continues in this building's sinews and ribs. The students who pedal 40 "ReRev" exercise elliptical machines will generate electricity fed back into the grid.

Good for them. I'll be at the smoothie bar!

What matters most is that this expansion is designed for students. We have added much more cardio equipment, a personal training studio, and a 1/9-mile indoor track upstairs.

We want students to be healthy while they are at UF, but we have a much bigger responsibility. This building, and this corner of campus, make a noble attempt at meeting that responsibility: that our students leave the University of Florida with a lifelong appreciation for learning, for health, for the natural world.

In Support of the College of Liberal Arts and Sciences

Remarks at Convocation for the College of Liberal Arts and Sciences, October 4, 2007

I think you may have asked yourself in the past 12 months or so what is happening in your college. Owing to a major budget deficit, the College of Liberal Arts and Sciences has been through a tough period, one felt in every department and discipline. With open positions left unfilled, travel restricted, and ordinary supplies suddenly hard to come by, it has been a painful time for faculty. Students have faced difficulty getting into certain courses.

I do not intend to rehash the circumstances that created this situation, nor do I want to try to recast it.

What I want to tell you is simply this: I strongly believe in CLAS's mission at the University of Florida, and in the value of a liberal arts education in general. I also want to say that although hardships continue, the CLAS budget deficit is shrinking fast, and the college is on the move.

I pledge to do all I can to ensure that this new dawn continues, and that CLAS has a bright future at the University of Florida.

Even with no budget deficit, it's hard to be the College of Liberal Arts and Sciences, circa 2007, and harder still for the basic sciences, liberal arts, and social sciences that are the college's mainstays. That's because there is so much emphasis in society, in Florida, and admittedly at this university on the professional schools and the training they provide.

Many taxpayers, not to mention politicians, want to see university education in the simplest possible light—as a sort of industrial process, taking in raw material in the form of high school graduates and graduating them four to five years later as salary earners. To this way of thinking, or perhaps non-thinking, universities exist only to add value to a product, the product being the professional consumer class.

Public appreciation for basic sciences and the social sciences is equally superficial.

Most people value university research, but as with graduates, they want a defined outcome with a readily understandable application. You might be able to convince them that basic science is important because it pays dividends down the road—that out of this apparently incomprehensible research they'll one day get faster computer chips, better running shoes, or the iPhone. But forget about trying to justify the more abstruse sciences and scholarly pursuits. To these eyes, studying theoretical physics, philosophy, or William Blake appears an expensive luxury.

I have the deepest respect for the professional schools, their graduates, and the applied research they do. I think it's remarkable, for example, that we can transform teenagers into engineers in a few short years, a feat we accomplish with roughly 850 students annually. And I think it's wonderful that researchers not only in the professional schools, but also in CLAS, come up with technologies and processes that have a ready value. The University of Florida is a national leader in technology transfer and commercialization, and that's something we should all be proud of.

But there is much, much more to a university education than training. And there is much, much more to university research than stocking the shelves of Best Buy with the latest electronics in time for the holiday season.

We are here not only to jump-start students in their professions, but to give them a well-rounded and deep education, one that prepares them as much as possible to be active and knowledgeable participants in our democracy. And we are here not only to innovate, but also to extend the boundaries of science and knowledge purely for their own sake.

These twin missions go back to the original charter of universities. But they are far from dated. To the contrary, a well-rounded education and an eagerness to pursue the fundamental questions of nature and science are more important than ever. In the past 20 years (1987–2007), 18 Nobel Laureates were educated at predominantly undergraduate institutions. Environments like that in CLAS.

The College of Liberal Arts and Sciences has many vital roles at the University of Florida. CLAS is home to virtually all of our undergraduates for the first two years of college. Here at CLAS, University of Florida students learn the writing, critical thinking, and quantitative skills essential to their success in the upper division. Not to mention seemingly mundane but critical practical skills such as good study habits and getting around the libraries.

Perhaps most importantly, CLAS students get the opportunity to explore, to get a taste of what's out there, and to try new things.

Many students arrive at UF believing that they will go pre-med or pre-law. We don't need that many lawyers or doctors! And fortunately, most of these students discover they are really more interested in something they never even heard of before they arrived at UF. Credit for this transformation goes to the rich variety of courses at CLAS. This is not just good for the students. It's what college is all about.

But CLAS does much more than take our newest and least experienced students under its wing. As I alluded to earlier, the true role of the liberal arts education is deeper, more expansive—and as it turns out, more urgent.

The Association of American Colleges and Universities published a fascinating report on liberal arts education earlier this year. One of the main thrusts is that today's university graduates are entering a disruptive if not chaotic world, one characterized by uncertainty and rapid change. In this era of global change, giving students a narrow training in a specific field does them a disservice.

The AAC&U says, and I quote, "Graduates will need to be intellectually resilient, cross-cultural and scientifically literate, technologically adept, ethically anchored and fully prepared for a future of continuous and cross-disciplinary learning."

In other words, graduates need the classically broad benefits of a liberal education now more than ever. And it's not just the AAC&U saying this. From Intel to State Farm to Raytheon, numerous industry leaders have extolled the virtues of employees with liberal arts backgrounds.

What's more, a liberal education doesn't just look good on one's résumé. The searching, skeptical frame of mind cultivated in the liberal arts is key to the vitality of our democracy. The same goes for much of what is taught as part of a liberal education—history, sociology, language. Again, there is renewed urgency about this: six years after 9/11, you have to be blind not to grasp the poverty of our understanding of the Middle East and the desperate need for more people educated in the languages and customs of that part of the world.

If questioning is the lifeblood of democracy, it is also essential to good science. Again, the College of Liberal Arts and Sciences is where students learn to adopt this mental stance, and where faculty may most freely pursue pure and basic questions.

And all the evidence is that our faculty do well at this: this year, CLAS brought in $48 million in research grants, up from $40 million last fiscal year, and two CLAS faculty members netted this university's first-ever grants from the Howard Hughes Medical Institute.

So I deeply value the College of Liberal Arts and Sciences and its important work of nurturing our most inexperienced students, upholding liberal arts, and probing the toughest and most basic scientific questions. Because I so value it, I am happy to see CLAS emerge from the significant budget constraints it has been under.

There are several pieces of good news for the college.

First, CLAS will be back in the black by next academic year, at least one year ahead of schedule. I know this required deep and lasting sacrifices throughout the college, but the results speak for themselves.

Second, a search committee has been formed and is soliciting nominations for a new dean. Third, we have set aside for the college four of five positions we are now recruiting despite a university-wide hiring freeze—one each in botany, chemistry, English, and psychology. We have also transferred enrollment management to CLAS, a step that brings significant additional resources for the college.

Last, we are protecting CLAS from most of the budget cutbacks being experienced elsewhere in the university due to the current state budget ills.

There is a certain irony in what's happening: CLAS is coming out of its budget problems just as everyone else is going into them. That is positive for the college, but at the same time, I know much more is needed.

Unfortunately, we have a deep-seated and long-standing funding problem. UF's tuition is the lowest in the country, and while this makes our university affordable it also shortchanges us compared to our counterparts in other states. All signs are that Florida is entering an era of budget shortfalls, which may only make a bad situation worse.

So the university is in a difficult position. However, it is not necessarily an intractable one. We made some progress this past spring when the Florida Legislature approved the state's first-ever differential tuition program. Starting next academic year, this program will allow UF to charge more than other state universities, which will allow us to begin to hire additional faculty members and advisors. The focus will be on the high-demand undergraduate areas of concentration. Many of these hires will be in the College of Liberal Arts and Sciences.

Meanwhile, just last week we launched our next major capital campaign, setting a goal of $1.5 billion. And we recently completed our Faculty Challenge campaign, raising over $200 million for faculty needs and resources in CLAS and elsewhere.

Progress won't be immediate, but it will come.

A particular concern for me is the resource needs of the humanities and social sciences. These disciplines encounter a large undergraduate teaching load and have limited resources to grow and adapt to new challenges.

Going forward, as a new point of emphasis in the Florida Tomorrow Campaign, I am announcing today the Humanities and Social Sciences Challenge. My goal is for $30 million in new endowment resources for these disciplines. We expect to focus just like we did for the Faculty Challenge. The new dean will assume major responsibility for allocating these funds. My hope is to recognize faculty with endowed professorships and to enhance graduate education with first-year and dissertation fellowships. In the end, this is not a lot of money and will not meet all our needs. It will take some time, perhaps the five years of the Florida Tomorrow Campaign.

To get the challenge started, today I am announcing a $1 million allocation to endow a professorship in English literature. I hope we could commence searching for the position soon. I am also announcing a $1 million endowment for graduate fellowships in psychology. This represents a $2 million beginning to the Humanities and Social Sciences Challenge.

Earlier in this speech I said that one of CLAS's greatest contributions is giving students the opportunity to explore. I want to return to this theme briefly in my closing.

Universities are fertile places for discovery, whether with regard to science, scholarship, or technology. But for many students, self-discovery is the most meaningful legacy of attending college. This can be an awfully painful process, but we emerge from it strengthened and better prepared for life ahead. Of course students can experience this transformation anywhere, but it is most likely to occur during that period of introspection, questioning, and exploring in the College of Liberal Arts and Sciences.

People learn who they are here, and that is a rare gift. I look forward to seeing this tradition continue as the college grows and prospers.

People before Politics

Remarks at the dedication of the Bob Graham Center
for Public Service, March 5, 2008

We are here to dedicate the Bob Graham Center for Public Service, but I want to begin with a few words about Bob Graham, the man.

Senator Graham served two terms as Florida governor, from 1979 to 1986. He was elected U.S. Senator for three terms, from 1987 to 2005. He is the former chairman of the Senate Intelligence Committee, a book author, and a rancher.

He has also been a bricklayer, shrimp fisherman, tomato picker, flight attendant, and Christmas elf.

Dozens of framed photos of Senator Graham, on the job in his trademark "workdays," cover the wall as you enter the Graham Center upstairs. In fact, it's only when you step into Senator Graham's office do you see photos of him with luminaries like President Clinton, President Carter, and longtime New York City mayor Ed Koch.

Bob Graham has always put people at the core of politics. That is also the guiding principle of the Bob Graham Center for Public Service.

As a popular governor, Bob Graham is remembered for improving public school student achievement, presiding over a strong state economy, and especially for protecting environmentally sensitive lands. As a senator, his achievements include launching our nation's project to restore Everglades National Park, protecting Florida's coast from oil drilling, and helping to redirect America's intelligence apparatus.

In Florida and nationally, Senator Graham was always a proud moderate. A Democrat loyal to his party, he was happy to sponsor bills with Republican colleagues.

When lifetime politicians retire, they often write memoirs. But I think this center, and its companion, at the University of Miami, represent Senator Graham's attempt to leave a more enduring legacy—one that he hopes will continue his brand of deliberative and measured statesmanship in an era that cries for it.

But before I get into all that, let me tell the story where it begins, right here at the University of Florida. Graham arrived as a freshman in 1955 and promptly ran for president of his class.

The politicos in the room will remember that he often said he never lost an election. Well . . . technically, as they say, that's not quite the case, because he lost that first race. But, Graham quickly ran for Freshman Honor Court, improving his strategy with a campaign poster that featured a large portrait of Abraham Lincoln.

It was spin, circa 1955. As Graham said later, "The hook was that people would say, 'who the hell is this guy who has got Abraham Lincoln on his poster?'"

Graham won, and a political career was born. He graduated UF in 1959, went to Harvard Law School, was elected to the Florida House of Representatives and then to governor and senator.

He is without a doubt both UF's most prominent graduate and Florida's best known and most successful politician.

A couple of other important things happened here at the University of Florida.

Graham met what he once remembered as a quote-unquote "stunningly beautiful brunette" who told him she needed some help with a science class.

He and Adele fell in love, married and went on to have four daughters. Three of them—Cissy Graham, Suzanne Gibson, and Kendall

Elias—grew up to attend and graduate from UF. Grandchildren followed. All told, at least 16 members of the family have attended UF.

Graham also made friends with Jim Pugh, a fellow Sigma Nu fraternity member. A half century later, that friendship was one of the catalysts for Mr. Pugh's donation to create this one-of-a-kind building, just dedicated a few weeks ago.

Which brings me back to the Graham Center.

When Graham earned his political chops, there was an informal network of business and political leaders that took aspiring young politicians under their wing.

In today's more cynical times, that network has, to an extent, disappeared. I think the senator will probably say more about this in his address, but I believe he wanted to re-create in a more formal setting the culture that nurtured his own rise. Senator Graham was also influenced by Harvard University's Kennedy School of Government, where he spent a year after his final term as Senator.

The University of Florida was the obvious choice. College of Liberal Arts and Sciences faculty had advocated for a public service center for some time. And so, urged on by former CLAS dean Neil Sullivan, the Graham Center was born.

Public service has lost much of the esteem it once enjoyed, with the result that the bright people starting their careers often look elsewhere. And yet we need their talent now more than ever.

I believe the Graham Center will help to recruit and to sharpen that talent, and the result will be better, more effective leaders.

Also, Florida is a young state, one that has never invested deeply in its universities. Our faculty are superb, and our students excellent. But because of these circumstances we chronically fall short not only in recognition, but more importantly in opportunities. This center will help to shift that historical momentum in a new direction.

Already, the change is palpable. Famed historian David McCullough spoke here last night. Senators Chuck Hagel and Jay Rockefeller will be here tomorrow.

I believe these leaders will come away from their visits with a new appreciation for UF and what we do here. And it's obvious that students who take the opportunity to get close to these speakers have much to gain.

The fact is, all great public universities have a noted public policy center. Now, we join them. And maybe this year, or maybe the year after that, the next Bob Graham will walk through these doors.

Thinking Deeply in a Twitter World

Remarks at the doctoral degree commencement ceremony,
August 9, 2013

There is no greater honor for me as president than to speak to you on this special day. I'm sure you are excited. I hope you are proud. And after toiling for three or four years ... or six ... or ten ... I know you are relieved and, also eager, to tackle the future.

In my own early academic life, I had already left my alma mater, the University of Iowa, and was at work in Washington, D.C., when I formally received my PhD in educational psychology.

I began that doctorate as a dentist. Everything was lined up for my career in clinical practice. But along the way I learned to love teaching, and I wanted to know more about the science of teaching.

I had no idea that my doctorate would lead to a lifetime in higher education, including provost at the University of Michigan, president of the University of Utah, and nearly 10 years here at the University of Florida.

You might expect the moral of this story to be that if you follow your passion, you'll be a success. Well, that would have been a safe theme, but I'm betting you've already heard it a time or two. So, actually, the message I have for you is this ...

The world doesn't need your passion so much as it needs your depth of thought and your highly developed analytical and reasoning skills—the skills that got you to where you are today.

Now I've got nothing against passion. It's just that our world is currently suffering from a glut of it, what with various wars, the partisanship in our national government which has us paralyzed as a country . . . and especially the religious zealots in various parts of the world trying to impose their will.

What we are sorely lacking in today's world is reasoning, defined as "thinking coherently and logically—the drawing of inferences or conclusions from facts known and assumed." This is a skill that after all the years you have devoted to primary research, is your special forte as doctoral graduates.

I told you my story about earning my doctorate. What I hesitate to admit is, my own commencement occurred 39 years ago, in 1974.

I am not one to be nostalgic about the past. Having survived Nixon, the Vietnam War, Reaganomics, and even punk rock, I can say with some perspective that no era is without ignorance and bad taste.

However, I do think this time in our history has its own unique challenge and one that we don't talk about often enough. That challenge is to find a way to mitigate our technology-induced addiction and fixation on instant fulfillment. What we really need is . . . you know . . . actual thinking.

For example, it's a symptom of our times that a week or so ago, people were concerned about an Internet story that there will be no more blond women in 200 years because, quote, "the blond gene is going extinct." I am not making this up!

I love technology as much as anyone. In fact, I just upgraded to a new Blackberry Q10. It's such a big deal in my life.

Yet I share the feelings of those who worry about the impact of our ringtones, electronic voices, and incessant Twitter and Facebook updates—the technologies that feed the social media of our time.

In his book *The Shallows: How the Internet Is Changing the Way We Think, Read and Remember,* Nicholas Carr argues that Internet-connected technology is quote "literally rewiring our brains and inducing only superficial understanding."

I tend to agree. It's tough to teach a class when students are forever checking their devices . . . hard to hold a conversation when someone's phone ringtone lets out with "Baby" by Justin Bieber. It's more difficult, ultimately, to think through a thorny problem when one's device pulses with the latest Internet sensation.

A recent survey found that Americans spend 16 minutes of every hour online checking social media. We need less linking, more thinking.

The real problem is that our Internet weaknesses are just a symptom of a more general drift toward the instant and easy, and away from the sustained and difficult.

Many of you are headed off to become postdocs or take positions at universities. It may interest you to know, universities used to care a lot about making students well rounded, with a solid grasp of their society and globe.

That's still part of the conversation at some universities, including this one. But there's no question the push is on to prepare students for careers and get them in and out the door as quickly as possible.

There's a growing impatience with the idea that learning and contemplation are worthy ends in themselves. Have you read *War and Peace*? Stayed up all night debating politics? Have you had a serious conversation about art? People don't even grasp the need for such activities. They want utilitarian degrees with rapid rewards, like frequent flier miles.

In business, the quarterly report trumps the multiyear relationship with employees and customers. In health care, quick treatment gets better financials than long-term prevention. In Hollywood, moviemakers produce the sequel to the sequel, trusting in the knockoff over the original.

It's not just that we're losing the ability to think deeply. We're even losing our respect for thinking itself. How else do we explain today's strange phenomenon of willful ignorance? Willful ignorance is the enthusiastic denial, against mountains of evidence, of evolution and climate change.

As doctoral graduates, all your scientific and scholarly instincts and training are contrary to these trends.

You've spent years pursuing questions that led, not to easy and satisfying answers, but only to harder questions. You've hunted ferociously, and sometimes fruitlessly, for facts that are not retrievable via Google. You've written . . . and rewritten . . . and rewritten . . . not for quote "friends" or "followers," but for experts poised to pick apart your every word.

The degree you will earn today is your tangible reward. But the more valuable rewards are the intangibles associated with your degree.

Through your advanced training, you've grown to appreciate the certainty of incremental progress over the false hope of dramatic leaps. You've learned to eschew the sensational for the sober. And I sincerely hope you've felt the satisfaction of contributing to real discovery, of becoming part of a cause that is bigger than yourselves. The satisfaction that comes from true commitment to advancing knowledge.

Many of your forebearers began work that changed the world with their doctoral research.

Alan Turing's 1938 thesis, "Systems of Logic Based on Ordinals," is at the foundation of modern computer science. Whatever you think of Noam Chomsky's politics, no one questions that his 1955 dissertation, "Transformational Analysis," revolutionized our understanding of the origins of human language.

Jane Goodall's 1965 thesis, "Behavior of the Free-Ranging Chimpanzee," set the stage for her path-breaking contributions to modern understanding of other primates. And Kate Millet's *Sexual Politics*, a cornerstone of the women's movement of the 1970s, took root as her PhD thesis.

Whether any of your dissertations will prove similarly earth- or consciousness-shaking remains to be seen. But there's no question that, as you prepare to leave this university, this Twitter world needs your proven powers of reason and depth more than ever.

If you're earning your degree in engineering or agriculture, we need you to restore the balance between economic growth and natural resource depletion.

We need you to slow climate change while adapting to its inevitable impacts. And to balance technological progress with solutions rooted in living with nature.

If you're graduating from the College of Liberal Arts and Sciences, we need historians to explain the complexities and contradictions of politics today by drawing out the hidden lessons of yesterday.

We need astronomers to inform our understanding of our planet through better understanding of other planets. And we need religion scholars to help us pave the treacherous road to peaceful coexistence of faiths.

If you are earning your degree from the College of Education, we need you to help our public schools lessen the disadvantages of race and class through meaningful interactions with students.

I'd love to discuss the great challenges facing all the graduates today, but I really need to check my phone.

Seriously, I hope I've made my point clear. We live in an era of incredibly complex and important challenges. Yet as a society, we are less and less able to put forth the mental exertion needed to solve these challenges.

With your advanced degree, you are our backstop against this drift, our champions of thinking over linking, our standard-bearers for the best use of the human mind—the power of reasoning. I hope you will make the most of that capacity because real human progress, as opposed to the virtual kind, depends on you.

3

Equality and Education

A Long Staircase to Equality

Remarks to the Association of Black Alumni on the 50th anniversary of the integration of the University of Florida, August 20, 2008

Usually when I speak to alumni groups, I look out into the audience and see a few elderly people who look like they received their bachelor's degrees before I did—a long time ago! But, there's no one like that today.

We have no septuagenarian or octogenarian black alumni who earned diplomas as young men and women. Why? This is the legacy of segregation. Until a half century ago this fall, black students were forbidden from attending the University of Florida.

With Barack Obama becoming the first African American to receive a major political party's nomination for president, this week is a watershed moment in black history. Senator Obama's nomination is a leap up a long staircase that starts with the slave ships, winds through the Civil Rights era, and climbs skyward from here.

Brave people have singled themselves out to climb each step up that staircase—including students right here at the University of Florida and alumni right here in this room today.

It took a lot of courage to come to UF in the late 1950s and early '60s, when UF was still a traditionally southern institution in a small southern town.

Fraternities paraded in Confederate uniforms at homecoming. The Alachua County courthouse had segregated water fountains.

The first black students threatened the "southern way of life." To come to UF, they had to have conviction and grit.

When George Allen was standing in line to register for classes, another student walked up and said, "Move out of the way, boy." Mr. Allen knocked him down, jumped on his chest, and told him, "Do not ever call me boy, do you understand?" He was tough!

When Stephan Mickle arrived on campus, no one spoke to him, and no one would sit by him at lunch or in class. He remembered, and I quote, "I did not intend for them to see me sweat. You wanted someone to speak to you and be friendly and talk, and that just did not happen."

Mr. Allen became UF's first black graduate when he earned a degree from the law school in 1962. Three years later, Stephan Mickle became our first black student to earn a bachelor's degree. Other brave students broke the color barrier in other colleges and, eventually, in the UF athletic program.

These brave, tough young people persisted against a racist culture and institution. They changed our campus and they changed our nation.

This year's celebration is important and appropriate. But, I am reminded as I stand here today that there are more steps to climb on the staircase.

We have become a more racially diverse institution. But anyone who tours our campus can see that it does not match the colors of our country.

We have reached out to more students from poor backgrounds or families not headed by professionals with college degrees. But the reality is that most of our students are middle-class or privileged.

We have created full scholarships, stepped up outreach, and are recruiting in urban high schools. But it's clear we need to do more.

This is an issue of fairness and equal access to education. But it goes deeper than that. We must give University of Florida students the chance to get to know peers of different races, cultures, and American experiences.

It is part of our duty of providing a well-rounded education, one that will serve students for a lifetime in a diverse country.

George Allen was accepted to the Harvard, Berkeley, and UF law schools. He chose to come here to UF because, in his words, "That was where all the integration was going on, the agitation, the quest for equality."

Every other pioneer we celebrate this year made a similar choice—climbing a step that made life harder for them, but better for the rest of us. You should all be immensely proud to stand with them on this staircase.

A Model for All People

Remarks to the Women's Student Assembly, August 27, 2012

If you are like me, you spent some time earlier this month watching the Olympics. I am so proud of the Gator women and men who together brought home 21 medals, more than Canada and Spain. However, I was most awed and inspired by another woman Olympian.

She was not a Gator. She was not an American. She was not even a medal winner.

This summer, Wojdan Shaherkani became the first woman to

compete in the Olympics from Saudi Arabia, a kingdom that bans girls and women from participating in sports. You may have missed her on the judo mat; she lost her match in just 90 seconds. But her name will live forever in the history books.

Ms. Shaherkani is a model for all people, women and men, who make the courageous choice to take a stand for fairness and equality in their societies. While women in this country enjoy far more equality than those in Saudi Arabia, she is an inspiration for all of us to take a stand for our own remaining inequities—whether on campus or in the larger American culture and institutions.

It is interesting that we are meeting here in Smathers Library. This building was completed in 1949, which is just two years after UF became coeducational, in 1947.

In other words, it has only been 65 years since this institution began accepting women—two generations. Much has changed for the better in that time.

Compared with the trickle of women on campus in the first years of coeducation, today, about 60 percent of UF students are women.

Where there were few female top administrators mid-century, we are proud to have many standout women leaders today.

Four UF vice presidents are women. Our police chief is a woman. We have several women deans, including in engineering, our most male-dominated college. This fall, one of our star journalism alumni, Diane McFarlin, becomes dean of the College of Journalism and Communications.

If women have made great strides in academics at UF, so too, they stand out in Gator athletics.

This academic year marks the 40th anniversary of Title IX equity in sports legislation—and, not coincidently, the 40th anniversary of the first official year of women's athletics at UF. In 1972–73, this university had five competitive women's sports. Today, we have 12.

UF leads all SEC universities, with 109 women's team titles. Female athletes such as swimmer Dara Torres are among the most famous and beloved of all Gator athletes.

Enrollment, university leadership, sports. . . . My wife, Chris, and I have been around long enough to remember the status of women prior to the equity movements of the 1960s and '70s, and we deeply appreciate these steps forward.

But while we are certainly enrolling enough women, we are not necessarily ensuring all reach their full academic and career potential. UF shares with other universities a failure to attract sufficient numbers of women to science, technology, engineering, and math majors—the so-called "STEM" disciplines. Female students may compose nearly 60 percent of our undergraduates, but they account for only 40 percent of our STEM majors.

We also need more women to seek terminal degrees and join the ranks of the faculty, both here at UF and nationally. Of about 5,000 professors at UF, almost 2,000 are women. This is an obvious shortcoming when the majority of these professors' students are women!

What matters most is that UF women have the support and encouragement to follow their dreams wherever they lie.

Regardless of your path here, the farther you take it, the greater the stand you take for women in spirit of Ms. Shaherkani and in the great tradition of UF alumnae . . . including Martha Barnett, the first woman president of the American Bar Association . . . noted feminist Eleanor Smeal . . . Weather Channel meteorologist Stephanie Abrams . . . former EPA administrator Carol Browner, and many, many others.

As we begin this academic year, let us not forget Ms. Shaherkani's challenges and her stand. And let us continue to take our own stand toward progress for all women at the University of Florida, in our nation, and on this planet.

A Story Worth Telling: The History of UF
Women before Coeducation

Remarks at the Women's History Month Awards Reception,
March 27, 2012

This year marks the 25th anniversary of the designation of Women's History Month. Your theme of "Making History Ours" reminds us that history has too often been recorded, studied, and written as half-history.

We know, for example, that the University of Florida became a coeducational institution in 1947, and we know that women here have a rich history of leadership and accomplishment after that date.

But 1947 was not the beginning of the history of women at the University of Florida. Just as women helped to shape Gainesville from its earliest days, so women have been a part of UF since it originated in 1853 in Ocala as the East Florida Seminary—a coeducational institution!

In the spirit of Women's History Month and "Making History Ours," I want to tell you a few things about what historians have learned about women at UF before coeducation in 1947.

- While UF may not have had women students, we certainly had women faculty. UF's first female regular faculty member may have been Ida Mai Lee, an assistant professor of chemistry. Dr. Lee's name appears in UF's 1918 course catalog.

- Although women could not attend UF during the regular school year, they were allowed to attend summer school, and did so from UF's earliest years in Gainesville. As a result, Mary Alexander Daiger became UF's first female graduate in 1920—27 years before UF officially began accepting women!

- A three-term letterman named Robert Swanson wrote "We are the boys from old Florida" in 1919. That is the stuff of UF legend. Less well known is that Robert's mother, Mrs. S. J. Swanson, was one of UF's first employees after the university opened in Gainesville in 1906.

- In 1924, Stella Biddle became the first woman to apply to the UF College of Law, but she was denied admission because of her gender. The dean, however, allowed her to attend classes as a visitor so that she could take the Florida Bar. Stella Biddle passed the Bar that same year.

- The first edition of *The Florida Alligator* was published in the summer of 1915. Four of the editors and one of the two circulation managers were women. Also that summer, at least four of the nine officers in UF student government were women.

- Although white women were admitted to UF beginning in 1947, that privilege was not extended to black women. It was another 12 years before Daphne Duval became UF's first black female student in 1959.

These are just a few of the stories in *Women at the University of Florida*, a book published by the University of Florida in 2003. The book's authors are Mary Ann Burg, Kevin McCarthy, Phyllis Meek, Constance Shehan, Anita Spring, Nina Stoyan-Rosenzweig, and Betty Taylor.

Phyllis Meek is here with us tonight. Phyllis, would you raise your hand? Would everyone join me in applauding Phyllis?

Phyllis helped give voice to the history of women at UF in the book I've quoted from. And she has been a key part of that history, working on gender equity for the campus and the nation since well before there was such a thing as Women's History Month.

Today, both society and the university have made enormous progress on women's issues—indeed, a majority of college students nationwide are women.

But we still do not have enough women in engineering or the sciences. We still do not have enough women faculty members. And we have not resolved other important issues, such as equality of compensation and the impacts of child bearing on tenure.

With that in mind, let me end with the pledge that as we push to give women their full credit in history, we will continue the crucial work of the present to ensure equality at UF and throughout the world.

I stand beside you in this all-important work—and I offer my deepest congratulations to all of tonight's award winners!

A Striking Symmetry

Remarks at the opening ceremonies for
Kathryn Chicone Ustler Hall, September 29, 2006

This building we are dedicating today, the Kathryn Chicone Ustler Hall, has been beautifully renovated and redesigned. But let us recognize it is important for reasons that go beyond bricks and mortar.

It is central to this university's history. And it is vital to our future.

Completed in 1919, this was the university's first real gym and assembly hall—our first building designed to be enjoyed by everyone. That brought a sense of community and shared purpose to a campus that was barely over a decade old.

Old photographs show this building all alone, shadowed only by longleaf pines. A field nearby remains a field to this day, but a very different one indeed: Florida Field.

Such was the need and desire for a gym and gathering place that Gainesville's residents even pitched in, donating the funds needed to overcome a budget shortfall to get the building completed. That's worth remembering this year, as the university celebrates its 100th anniversary in Gainesville.

Everyone called the building the "new gym" because it replaced UF's original exercise room in Thomas Hall. There was so much enthusiasm that UF's president and Gainesville's mayor invited the

New York Giants here for spring training. The team came that spring of 1919—but only after UF agreed to install showers!

In later years, the Giants moved on to other spring training grounds, but I am sure our athletes continued to appreciate those showers.

Architectural fans will note this building's expansive windows, so skillfully integrated into brick arches and buttresses. These windows were designed to provide ventilation in the years before air conditioning, while also exposing the clear span of the basketball court.

For many years, this place was the heart of the University of Florida. The two biggest events on the social calendar each year, fall and spring frolics, were held here. The dances were so popular that there was a lottery to attend, with the band playing two complete sets for two entirely different crowds of revelers.

After the university began admitting women in 1948, the new gym became the Women's Gymnasium. The name endured even as the building slowly fell into disuse and disrepair. As Neil mentioned, the Women's Gym sat empty for 27 years, its proud history slipping into obscurity.

Six years ago, Kathryn Chicone Ustler came to its rescue.

Kay is a great friend to the University of Florida who comes from a family of great friends to this university. She is a UF alumnus, a 1961 graduate with a degree in sociology. It won't surprise you to know that she believes strongly in the importance of historic preservation and has been active in preservation efforts in her home of Orlando.

As a university, we cannot know where we are going unless we know where we have been. So in preserving this building, so central to fostering the university's sense of itself as a warm and welcoming community, Kay has helped preserve our past and our purpose.

For that invaluable gift, I want to thank Kay and her son, Craig, who has also contributed. I also want to pay tribute to the Chicone family, who have been committed and valued supporters of the university's athletic program for many decades.

There is a symmetry about the Kathryn Chicone Ustler Hall that is striking. It is the former Women's Gym. Its restoration is sponsored by a woman. It is UF's first academic center to be named exclusively after a woman. And, of course, the Kathryn Chicone Ustler Hall will serve as home to the university's women's studies programs.

In that capacity, this building so vital to our history will also remain central to this university's future.

The field of women's studies is an essential component of any large research university, and that's certainly true at the University of Florida. Virginia Woolf wrote famously of the need for a woman to have a "room of her own." While I think we have made great strides since Woolf's era, I believe it remains important to give women's studies a nurturing home, one that fosters both lively conversation and great scholarship.

With its sunlit classrooms and offices, its libraries and galleries and its garden, Ustler Hall will do all that and more. I know that all of you share in my pride today as we dedicate the Kathryn Chicone Ustler Hall.

"Arouse the Conscience of the Nation"

Remarks in celebration of Martin Luther King Day,
the Presbyterian and Disciples of Christ Student Center,
January 22, 2008

So much can be said about Dr. King's vision, and the important struggle that he led, that one hardly knows where to begin.

But since we are gathered here at the Presbyterian and Disciples of Christ Student Center, I thought I would focus my brief remarks on Dr. King's legacy as it relates to youth, and especially to college students.

Students were at the epicenter of the civil rights movement. In

1960, four black students at North Carolina Agricultural and Technical College sat down to eat at a segregated Woolworth lunch counter in Greensboro, North Carolina. That action sparked similar sit-ins throughout the South, and is viewed today as a pivotal moment in the struggle.

A year later, black and white college students organized the Freedom Rides challenging segregation on buses and in bus terminals. Many freedom riders were badly injured by violent mobs, but the protests led President Kennedy to ban segregation in interstate busing.

News reports and photos of violence against the students also helped swing the national mood in favor of the civil rights agenda.

Gainesville avoided the worst rioting and violence of the era, but students played a key role here as well. Among them was Virgil Hawkins, whose rejected 1949 application to the UF law school led to the desegregation of Florida's entire university system.

I am told this very Presbyterian student center served as a gathering point and safe haven for an early group of black students seeking admission to the university in the early 1960s.

Martin Luther King had his differences with student activists—he thought the Freedom Rides were too dangerous—but he was the first to recognize that college students were at the center of his struggle.

Shortly before he was assassinated in 1968, King said that when black students "took their struggle to the streets, a new spirit of resistance was born. Inspired by the boldness and ingenuity of Negroes, white youth stirred into action and formed an alliance that aroused the conscience of the nation."

Today, I think that all of us, but especially the students present here tonight, can honor King's legacy by taking those words to heart.

Forty years after his death, many people in this country continue to face discrimination, injustice, threats to their constitutional rights, poverty, or hunger. All of you, too, can "arouse the conscience of the nation."

In Praise of Stephan P. Mickle

Remarks at a reception for Federal Judge Stephan P. Mickle,
the first black student to earn an undergraduate degree from UF,
March 28, 2008

A half century after the first black students walked through the doors at the University of Florida, we are a much more diverse institution—and much richer for it. We owe a great debt to these students, including the man we honor tonight, Stephan P. Mickle.

Any member of the judiciary who rises from lawyer to federal judge has achieved a lot.

But to appreciate U.S. District Court judge Mickle's career and influence on our campus and state, we need to consider what times were like when he arrived at this university in September 1962, joining 13,826 students—nearly all of them white.

Judge Mickle recalled his experience in an oral history recorded some years ago. It is a rich document. Let me share a couple of details with you.

All new students are nervous and self-conscious about the impression they make on their peers. Appreciate, for a moment, Stephan Mickle's predicament.

As he recalled in the oral history, when he waited in line to register for classes, no one spoke to him. When he sat down in class, it was almost a sure thing no one would sit in the desk next to him. Walking across campus, he worried constantly about insults or provocations.

In his words, and I quote, "I did not intend for them to see me sweat, as the saying goes. You wanted someone to speak to you and be friendly and talk, and that just did not happen."

UF did not experience the level of racial violence seen at the University of Mississippi and other universities, but everyone here knew the quote-unquote "proper order of things." Certain fraternity members still dressed in Confederate uniforms during homecoming. The Alachua County courthouse had separate water fountains.

But with the civil rights struggle in full bloom elsewhere, there was also change in the air here. Progressive students and faculty, though by no means the majority, were a presence on campus, and they found Stephan Mickle, or vice versa.

He majored in political science and, in 1965, became the first black person to earn an undergraduate degree from UF.

He went on to earn his master's degree in a single year. After a year teaching high school in Brevard County, he returned to UF, entering the law school in fall of 1967.

Only two other black students, George Starke and George Allen, had attended the law school before him. In his oral history, Stephan Mickle recalls that he had never met a single black lawyer in his life! And yet here he was with all white students, many of whom had fathers or grandfathers who were lawyers or judges.

Stephan Mickle's parents, Andrew and Catherine, were both career educators, and they had done a terrific job because, despite the obvious hardships, their son did fine.

As occurs to this day, a lot of law professors demanded that students speak publicly in class. In that environment, Stephan Mickle's abilities became clear quickly enough, and that helped to win him acceptance among his peers.

Grades were posted, and his solid performance also helped. And while the old guard persisted, the quote-unquote "liberal" students and professors accepted and encouraged the budding young attorney.

One of the young faculty members Stephan Mickle became close to was Fletcher Baldwin. Together, Judge Mickle and Professor Baldwin began an effort to bring other black students to the law school, visiting Bethune-Cookman and other black colleges on informal recruiting trips. It was thanks to those trips and a 1971 summer program in Fort Lauderdale that the first sizable group of black students— eight or ten students—enrolled in the UF law school.

Such was Stephan Mickle's impression on his fellow students that he was elected vice president of his graduating class of 1970.

Later that year, he became the second black student to graduate, beginning a career marked by several impressive "firsts." Ten years ago this year, following a nomination by President Bill Clinton, Stephan Mickle was named U.S. District Judge for the Northern District of Florida.

Judge Mickle and his courageous peers left several important legacies.

One, they blazed a trail for others to follow. More than four decades after he and six others broke the color barrier in our undergraduate program, the university has graduated upwards of 12,000 black students. By no means are we as diverse as we should be, but we are working on it. I hope and trust that those black students who are here today experience a much different place than did Judge Mickle.

At least as importantly, Judge Mickle and his fellow pioneers made UF a better university—and this country a better, stronger nation.

I use the word "better" in the most general and expansive sense. It seems obvious today that we cannot block a class or race of people from participating if we expect to grow and prosper. This is true in society, and it is true at this university.

Not only that. As people, we injure our humanity in discriminating against others, and we deny ourselves the richness of experience on this earth. We cannot be the nation we want to be, or the university we want to be, without everyone participating in equal measure. Judge Mickle helped bring about that equal participation, and for that we owe him a great debt.

Now Is the Time to Gather Our Memories

Welcome remarks at the Samuel Proctor Oral History
Collection Panel Discussion, March 17, 2009

Chris and I are glad to join you tonight. Joel Buchanan and the panelists with us have spent a lifetime researching, writing about, and, through their activism, *making* African-American history.

I am eager to hear their thoughts about their personal experiences, their discipline, and how President Obama's service influences their perspective.

I am also delighted to support the Samuel Proctor Oral History Collection in its efforts to ramp up the preservation and promotion of Florida black history. This public program is part of that campaign, and it is well timed.

Everyone nods to the importance of history, but why? Why care about doing history, African American or otherwise? I was thinking about this question, and I was reminded that we at the University of Florida did some history of our own last year—we celebrated the 50th anniversary of UF's integration.

It was surprisingly challenging. And yet, I think our experience left me with some insights about the deep value of historical inquiry.

Nineteen fifty-eight was, of course, the year that George Starke Jr. became UF's first black student when he enrolled in our law school. He was followed in short order by George Allen, the first to graduate from the law school, and Stephan Mickle, the first black student to earn an undergraduate degree. All are celebrated, as well they should be.

But the committee in charge of this year's commemoration wanted to also recognize the black graduates who integrated UF's *other* colleges.

Like Mr. Starke, Mr. Allen, and Mr. Mickle, most of these students experienced an unfriendly or indifferent campus. Some white students wouldn't speak to them. Some faculty were patronizing, or worse. Administrators were not always sympathetic.

It took courage to be black, to be 18 or 19, to be away from home, in this place!

Yet, when Florida Bridgewater-Alford, our community relations director, sought out these graduates' names, she kept coming up empty.

With a few notable exceptions, no one bothered to note the identities of the first black students to graduate their colleges. Fifty years on, it was like they had never been there.

You'd think ferreting out the names would be easy. Just check with the registrar. But, back then, no one recorded race on transcripts. Why should they? Everyone was white!

I won't detail all the committee's detective work, but it was considerable.

In the end, our historian, Carl Van Ness, literally scoured UF's old yearbooks in search of African American faces. Carl then attempted to cross-check the names beneath the yearbook pictures with university records.

As he is the first to admit, this method has gaping flaws. Physical features are often ambiguous when it comes to race. But there you have it.

In some cases, those who worked on this project were able to confirm that a student had, in fact, been the first black student to graduate his or her college. In others, we could determine only that a student was one of the first.

In any case, we wound up expanding the list of "firsts" from just a handful to, I am proud to say, *twenty* first black graduates.

When the committee contacted these graduates to invite them to a dinner and recognition in their honor, some expressed disbelief.

They were astonished that a university which had hosted them only reluctantly, under a cloud of institutionalized racism, would reach out a half century later.

At the time, some of these students felt so bad about their experience at UF they didn't attend their own graduation ceremony!

Doing history helps turn the page. It makes wrongs right. It allows people to move on.

Some of these graduates have since told their stories to UF oral historians. Their words join the words of others in the Florida black history collection.

What becomes clear when you consider this collection is that these memories constitute not just African American history, but American history.

These words recount experience that, whether black or white, we all share.

Does Barack Obama's election suggest we are overcoming this past? We can hardly answer that without having our history laid out before us as our guide and our reference. As George Santayana wrote, "A country without memory is a country of madmen."

My final insight from our 50th anniversary celebration is that it's important to do this history now, today. Because, otherwise, much of it will disappear.

It was hard enough to find our first black graduates and bring them to UF this year, five decades after they arrived. We won't have these people forever.

Nor will we have the many white and black Americans who joined the Freedom Rides, assembled for the "I Have A Dream" speech, who integrated the nation's other secondary schools and universities.

Now is the time to gather their memories—to add their stories to our story.

On that note, I am very pleased tonight to have the opportunity to present a special honor to a man who may have done more to preserve and celebrate local African American history than any other. He is my good friend Joel Buchanan.

Joel made his own history: he was the first black student to pass through the doors of Gainesville High School.

Through the years since, he continued his activism while also taking on the role of a beloved community caretaker.

In the early 1980s, long before Florida black history was on the radar, Joel gathered some 45 oral histories of local African Americans. His work can be found online today in the "Fifth Avenue Blacks" section of the digital collection.

Joel Buchanan has been recognized for his work with the Martin Luther King Jr. Keeper of the Dream Award and the Rosa Parks Silent Courage Award, among other awards.

Tonight, I would like to add our own symbol of appreciation.

Joel, will you join me here on stage so that I can give you a plaque.

The plaque reads, "The Samuel Proctor Oral History Program Recognizes Joel Buchanan. In honor of your work to preserve and promote African American History for Future Generations. March 17, 2009."

The Conscience of the Campus

Remarks at the 40th Anniversary Celebration of the UF
Institute of Black Culture, February 17, 2012

I am honored to join you to mark this 40th anniversary of the Institute of Black Culture. In the modern history of the University of Florida, few organizations have been as vital as the IBC.

Vital, because before the center was founded, black students attending this traditionally all-white university had nowhere to turn for support. Vital, because the IBC has offered a safe and familiar home for black students for four decades. And vital, because the IBC ended UF's heritage of excluding other races and cultures and launched its practice of celebrating them, inspiring other groups to do the same.

Like other southern educational institutions, UF refused to admit black students until forced into a corner by the courts. The university enrolled George Starke Jr. in 1958 but was in no hurry for transformative change. A decade after Mr. Starke entered the law school, UF had only 103 black students and four black professors.

The accumulating burdens of attending a university utterly indifferent to their needs steadily became too much for black students and faculty. In 1971, protests, arrests, and mass withdrawals rocked the campus.

Out of those tumultuous days came the seeds of real change, including the establishment in 1972 of the Institute of Black Culture.

Betty Shabazz was the celebrity keynote speaker at the grand opening, held 40 years ago this month. The Alligator reported that she spoke to a packed university auditorium "passionately and angrily" about the cruelties of slavery while extolling the contributions of black thinkers—and urging the center to uphold and honor black history and culture.

Ms. Shabazz said, quote, "I hope the center will show the necessity for international law, for warmth to show people they are brothers—especially blacks and blacks—and teach respect for black ancestors and a way of life."

The IBC has realized those hopes. Just as meaningful, it has inspired sister organizations to form in its image.

With Hispanic enrollment on the rise, La Casita, the Institute of Hispanic Latino Culture, opened in 1994. More recent arrivals are the Office of Lesbian, Gay, Bisexual, and Transgender Affairs and the Office of Asian Pacific Islander American Affairs.

A university that once rejected and repudiated people's racial and cultural identities today has a dedicated staff in Multicultural and Diversity Affairs to promote them.

The celebration of diversity has become a mantra of our campus. The IBC began this progress.

At a time when students arrive from around the globe, some with little knowledge of black history, the IBC's mission of championing black culture is only more essential. And, no matter how sensitive the university strives to be, it can still benefit from insight and course corrections from the IBC.

Forty years ago, the IBC was a catalyst for transformative change. Today, it serves as a conscience of our campus. I assure you we will listen to that conscience as we seek to make the University of Florida the best possible university for all students.

"The Only Queer People"

Remarks at the March Against Hate, organized in response to anti-gay vandalism at the UF law school, Turlington Plaza, September 20, 2012

I am so pleased and proud to see all of you gathered today in support of the values we hold dear—and in opposition to the hatred and intolerance we know is wrong, hurtful, and destructive.

Whatever shadow was cast by the deplorable incident at the law school . . . you bring the light . . . or perhaps I should say, you bring the rainbow!

The pioneering gay activist and former San Francisco mayor Harvey Milk once said, "All young people, regardless of sexual orientation or identity, deserve a safe and supportive environment in which to achieve their full potential."

I could not agree more, and I want to take this opportunity to reaffirm that the University of Florida is a university that welcomes people of all races, genders, cultures, and sexual orientations. That we do not accept intolerance, discrimination, or violence. And that we will not rest until the campus is a model of safety, decency, respect, and equality.

As a prominent public university and a respected institution of higher learning, what happens on our campus matters. We are a showcase to the country and the world, and it is important that we reflect and model the highest and best elements of the human spirit.

Bigots like to hurl names and epithets—but we know those names and epithets say more about the bigots than their intended targets.

As author, lesbian activist, Floridian, and onetime University of Florida student Rita Mae Brown once said so brilliantly, "The only queer people are those who don't love anybody."

I thank all of you for joining this march today to show all the true colors of the University of Florida and our campus community. And I urge all of you to keep raising your voices against bigotry and for acceptance and love.

4

Celebrating with Ceremony

9/11 and Roosevelt's Four Freedoms

Remarks at the 10th anniversary commemoration
of the September 11 attack at University Auditorium,
September 11, 2011

Welcome, members of the university and Gainesville communities. On the tenth anniversary of 9/11, it is heartening to be surrounded by people who care as deeply as you about our country, our community, and our campus.

Anyone who is old enough to remember 9/11 knows exactly where she or he was on that fateful morning. We didn't have to be near New York or Washington, D.C., or even know anyone affected by the terrible events there. At 8:46 A.M., when the first plane struck the North Tower of the World Trade Center, 9/11 instantly became permanent in each and every one of us.

The sense that our security had vanished, the anger and grief over the thousands who were killed, the fear of what might come next . . . 9/11/01 is deeply personal history. Today, as we recall where we were on that day, it may be of some comfort to think about what happened in the aftermath—and where we as Americans have come from.

As the magnitude of the attacks sank in, we were awed by the heroism of firefighters and police at the World Trade Center and the Pentagon. All around the country, and here at the University of Florida, Americans lined up to volunteer, to donate emergency funds, to give blood. In the space of one morning, we rediscovered our patriotism and national kinship.

That feeling of unity is one of the most powerful I have ever known. For me, it still counterbalances the horror of that day.

Within weeks, UF researchers were at Ground Zero, helping with engineering surveys, forensics, and crisis intervention for first responders and survivors. Everyone in the Gainesville community and on our campus wanted to help their country.

As time passed, we came to experience an America altogether different—and in some ways unrecognizable—from the one we knew before. Most of us here today are old enough to remember our country before this transformation.

But with every passing year, there are fewer of us. The 18-year-olds who enrolled at UF for the first time this fall were in third grade in 2001.

Soon, we'll have students with no memories of 9/11 or the America before the tragedy. Before long security lines at airports. Before endless debates about how to keep the country secure while protecting civil liberties. Before two deadly and costly wars in Iraq and Afghanistan that have drawn hundreds of brave UF students and alumni to combat.

So, on this tenth anniversary of 9/11, it seems to me we can continue to heal by thinking of our most treasured traditional values as Americans—values too precious to be taken from us by terrorists. In recalling these values, it may be helpful to think of the words of an earlier American leader in an era when the nation's security was also under threat.

In January 1941, most of Western Europe had fallen to Nazi domination, but Pearl Harbor was 11 months away and the U.S. had yet to enter the conflict. In his State of the Union address, President Franklin Delano Roosevelt strived to prepare Americans for a war he knew was inevitable, but that many in our country still wanted no part in.

In what has become known as his "Four Freedoms" speech, FDR spoke of an America committed to a world "founded upon four essential freedoms." Freedoms to which everyone is entitled. Those freedoms are freedom of speech, freedom of worship, freedom from want, and freedom from fear.

"That is no vision of a distant millennium," FDR said. "It is a definite basis for a kind of world attainable in our own time and generation."

This nation pursued FDR's vision of four freedoms successfully in World War II, and then again throughout the Cold War with the former Soviet Union. 9/11, the deadliest foreign attack on American soil ever, has posed the greatest test of our commitment. But universities and university communities, including the University of Florida and Gainesville, have always been sacred and safe houses for the four freedoms.

Here at UF, we have championed free speech, even when it has been unpopular. In this tolerant university community, we have a stunning diversity of religions, all worshiping peacefully. We are a caring community that always pitches in when there is need, whether from an earthquake in Haiti or a hurricane at home. As for the last freedom, freedom from fear, this university answers fear with education and understanding.

Let us balance our memories of *where we were* on 9/11/01 with the courage and faith in *who we are* as Americans. Whatever threats our country faces in the future, the freedoms we treasure on our campus and in this community will always help us prevail.

Our Newest and Truest History

Remarks at the grand opening of the First Colony Exhibit,
October 17, 2013

It was a little over three years ago that we joined hands in Historic St. Augustine. I think all of you would agree, we've done a lot to preserve this city's historic treasures and make them a magnet for tourism.

But I'm convinced the power of this partnership goes beyond buildings and visitors. The real power of this work lies in reclaiming . . . and proclaiming . . . our true history as a people and as a country. This is history we especially need to highlight this year, the 500th anniversary of Ponce de León's landing in Florida.

UF's Kathleen Deagan and her students began this work decades ago with their archaeological investigations. Supported by the Florida Museum of Natural History, Dr. Deagan and her students discovered the site of the original Spanish settlement—the first permanent European settlement in America—established in 1565.

Our country's true history further came to light in the scholarship of Michael Gannon and the legal and preservation work of Roy Hunt and Roy Graham. And it is embodied in the new First Colony Exhibit, which tells a story of native Floridians and Spanish Colonial Florida that has often been ignored.

As the exhibit makes clear, that ignored history includes the real first Thanksgiving in the U.S. In 1565, a meal was served that included pork, olives, and red wine. And here we've spent the last 400 years eating cranberry sauce!

President Harry Truman once said, "There is nothing new in the world except the history you do not know."

A lot of people do not know about the Timucua, who were the native peoples of this area. Or that the Spanish, and not the Pilgrims, were the first New World settlers. Or that St. Augustine preceded Jamestown, still wrongly regarded as America's first settlement, by 42 years.

So as we open our First Colony Exhibit revealing the story of oldest America, I am happy the University of Florida is joining all of you to reclaim ... and to proclaim ... our newest and truest history.

Our Debt to Student Veterans

Remarks at the dedication of the UF Veteran's Memorial at
the Reitz Union Amphitheatre, April 30, 2009

We recently bore witness to the incalculable value of our men and women in uniform when Navy Seals rescued an American captain from pirates off the coast of Somalia.

But, such an intense spotlight is rare.

American soldiers, including University of Florida students or recent graduates, risk their lives every day in Iraq, Afghanistan, and other parts of the world. They are too easy to overlook. I am very grateful to have this physical reminder of their service and their sacrifice.

It is hard to imagine, on this beautiful spring day, with the excitement of commencement so palpable across campus, that University of Florida students are fighting now, have fought in past wars, and have given their lives for their country.

In fact, military service is a campus tradition, one that dates to the early years of this university.

In 1917, when the United States entered World War I, 274 of the 434 men enrolled at what was then all-male UF, went to war.

It is estimated that as many as 10,000 UF students served in World War II. Many faculty also joined up, so the war had a radical impact on campus. By the peak year of 1944–45, UF had just 740 students, down from 3,500 before the fighting started.

The number of students who served in Korea, Vietnam, and more recent conflicts is less clear. But there is no question that hundreds of UF men and women were part of those wars as well.

Some never made it back. We lost 401 students to World War II alone.

The dead included Gator football players, student government officials, and other leaders. We don't always know it, but we still speak their names today. Corry Village is named after William Corry, one of two student body presidents killed.

All told, it is thought that as many as 700 UF students have been lost to war.

If UF has been a ready source of men and women sent to fight overseas, it has also been a place for them to come home to.

We had so many veterans enroll after World War II that we had to build three makeshift cities containing over 1,000 residences. The Flavet Villages went up so fast, they included travel trailers and re-used military barracks!

Today, we are proud to count around 1,000 veterans among our undergraduate and graduate students.

We owe a huge debt to all the brave students who gave their young lives for their country. We remember and honor them with this memorial.

But, this granite and steel is important for another reason: it serves as a reminder of our responsibilities with respect to the veterans who are current UF students.

Veterans are often older than typical students. They have been out of school longer, and many have experienced combat. Some may have to cope with physical challenges from injuries. All these factors make readjusting to civilian life difficult.

We can ease these students' paths with patience, empathy—and especially, with friendship.

As this memorial reminds us, we can also make clear that we understand and appreciate what these veterans chose to do for all of us.

Pioneering Education at P. K. Yonge

Speech at P. K. Yonge's 75th Anniversary Celebration,
June 27, 2009

On behalf of the University of Florida, I want to extend a warm welcome to each of you to P. K. Yonge Developmental Research School's 75th anniversary celebration.

These days, P. K. uses a lottery system for admission. But, for years and years, the waiting list to get into this school was legendary. It was common knowledge you had to sign up early—and I do mean early. New mothers, heading home from the hospital, would literally make a detour to P. K.'s admissions office to put their infants on the list for kindergarten.

When you understand this school's progressive roots . . . when you look into how it has influenced public education . . . when you get acquainted with its successful alumni . . . you know why families were, and are, still so eager to enroll their kids.

P. K. Yonge was that good! It *is* that good!

P. K. Yonge Laboratory School, as it was originally known, was established in 1934. From the outset, the school's missions were to give UF education students practical classroom experience, to test new ideas and practices in education, and to offer an alternative to Gainesville youth from kindergarten through 12th grade.

P. K. has done just that, with great success, for 75 years.

It's amazing how many of the concepts in education today that we take for granted made early appearances at P. K. Yonge. As far back as the 1930s, the school stressed problem-solving activities, group discussions, and student research, rather than lectures and worksheets.

Teachers urged students to interview people in the community and research primary sources in libraries.

The school has undergone many changes over the decades, consistently pioneering new ideas in education that later gained a far larger following.

A 1960s-era "adopt a grandparent" program foreshadowed mentoring programs that are common today. A developmental reading program launched in the early 1980s spread to school districts around the country. P. K.'s physical education program began offering young women the same opportunities as young men four years before Title IX was passed.

These were not just paper innovations. Real students benefited. You can see it in P. K.'s alumni, whose lives mirror the creativity of their education. Graduates range from an academy award–nominated film editor to an inventor of the Hubble Telescope to an international skateboard champion.

With so many interesting and accomplished alumni, and so many here in this room, I want to single out just one by name.

Here with us tonight is a member of P. K.'s class of 1938—its fourth graduating class. After earning a bachelor's and MBA from UF, this graduate became a tenured faculty member here—then went on to serve 24 years in the Florida House of Representatives and 12 years as a very highly regarded Florida Commissioner of Education.

Would everyone here please join me in recognizing a great man and the namesake for UF's own Turlington Hall, Ralph Turlington?

P. K.'s alumni are not the only evidence for its success.

Earlier, I mentioned the old waiting list system. The important addendum is that, years ago, P. K. began emphasizing diversity among its students, and in 2001 the school changed its policy to a lottery system to give students equal chance of acceptance. Today about 49 percent of P. K.'s 1,140 students hail from minority populations.

Student performance is impressive. P. K. is an "A" school—in fact, it has been one for the past seven years. Its graduation rate far eclipses the state average. Its visual, performing arts, and sports programs are known far and wide for their quality.

Let me conclude with a word or two about P. K.'s Yonge's future.

Recognizing the force of technology in reshaping our society, P. K. teachers are emphasizing the next generation of Internet applications in classrooms. The school has also begun efforts to retrofit its campus as a green campus, with the elementary school wing likely first in line.

P. K.'s fundamentals—a strong emphasis on writing, reading, and analytical skills, arts and music, coupled with physical activity and education—will always remain.

But, as ever, the school is on the educational vanguard. The University of Florida is fortunate to have such a wonderful ally in its research and education missions, just as the Gainesville community is lucky to have this unique alternative for its children.

Congratulations on your 75th! Many more to come!

The Enduring Legacy of Our Student Veterans

Remarks at the UF Student Veteran's Reception,
November 10, 2009

Much is said on Veteran's Day about the sacrifices of our men and women on the battlefield. This is as it should be. We owe everything—our country, our freedoms, our security—to our brave men and women in uniform in past and present conflicts.

But, here is something less often noted: veterans have done much more than defend our country. They have also reshaped it for the better.

We have a case in point right here in student veterans at the University of Florida.

Before World War II, education here, and at other public universities, was a privilege of the upper middle class and wealthy.

The GI Bill opened the door to students from far more modest backgrounds. They came by the busload! We had 3,500 students before the war. In 1947, we had 7,500. By 1950, enrollment reached

10,000. As a result of the influx of veterans, in other words, public education became truly "public."

Before the war, we were an all-male school. Veterans wanted their wives and girlfriends here, and young women wanted the same opportunities as men. As a direct result of veteran students, UF went co-ed in 1947. You see the same trends at many other public universities.

Veterans from this era—the quote-unquote "greatest generation"—went on to build the most prosperous, equitable, open country this world had ever seen.

Today, we think of a college education as an opportunity that everyone deserves. And we take for granted our country's large middle class. These are the legacies of our World War II student veterans. They made the most of the freedoms they fought for in Europe and the Pacific.

This legacy continued after the war, and continues today.

A country that asked its men to make the ultimate sacrifice could not continue to force black Americans into second-class citizenship. President Harry Truman ordered the military desegregated in 1948. Today, that order is seen as a first step toward racial equality in this country.

Many veterans were prominent leaders in the Civil Rights movement. Our own George Starke Jr. served in the Air Force. In 1958, Mr. Starke was the first black student to enter UF.

Veterans democratized higher education, built our economic prosperity, equalized our society. Our current 23.2 million veterans continue to enrich American life.

The story of Iraq and Afghanistan veterans has only just begun, but already they are making their influence known. For example, voters have elected at least four Iraq war veterans to Congress.

Many of you are skilled at working with people from vastly different cultures, tackling tasks as a diverse team, and handling jobs that are highly technical. These are precisely the skills America needs to pull out of its slump, compete globally, and spread our values.

President Obama said in a speech this year that GI Bill veterans produced three presidents, three Supreme Court justices, 14 Nobel Prize winners and two dozen Pulitzer Prize winners. I have no doubt your future will also see such achievement.

On this Veteran's Day, I want to thank you for all that you have done for your country—and all that you will do.

'Twas the Night before Christmas ... at UF

President Machen and First Lady Chris Machen give a lighthearted opening to the Sounds of the Season Concert each December. At the concert on December 4, 2011, President Machen donned a red sleeping cap and read this poem aloud.

'Twas the night before Christmas, when through Tigert Hall,
Not a paper was shuffling; they'd slowed to a crawl.

The VPs and their staff had locked up and gone out,
In hopes that Santa Albert would soon show his snout.

The students were nestled all snug in their beds,
As gingerbread lattés swirled in their heads.

Chris in her 'kerchief, and I in my cap,
Had just settled our brains for a warm Florida nap.

When out on Lake Alice there arose such a roar,
I sprang from my bed, most fearful of gore.

There, on the lake, as big as a freighter,
With eyes like headlights, a mammoth bull gator.

Not bearded, not jolly—but in his "Beat Ohio State" shirt,
I knew in a moment it was Santa Albert.

He was dressed in orange and blue, from his snout to his tail,
With mud on his claws thick as Gainesville Swamp Ale.

His big old eye winked, and his tail gave a slap,
Nudging me to reach into his pack.

I stuck my hand in, and pulled out, like a dream,
A national championship football team—maybe not this year!

I reached in again, and thought surely not,
When I yanked out an anthropology-loving Governor Rick Scott!

I poked my hand again in that magical store,
And students cried for tuition hikes: "more, more, more, more!"

Top rankings, faculty-student ratios ten-to-one,
My wishes spilled out, by the pound, by the ton!

Albert spoke not a word, but waggled his claw at me,
And I saw the error of my lame fantasy.

I realized we have everything we need to be great:
Our university, our community, the best in the state!

Our people, our nature, an overflowing bounty,
At UF, in Gainesville, and Alachua County.

Albert reared up, to his team he gave a bellow,
Back into Lake Alice they slogged, fat and mellow.

And I heard him exclaim, 'ere they swam out of sight,
Happy Holidays to all Gators and to all a good night!"

. . . Thank you! Welcome to the University of Florida and the Curtis
M. Phillips Center for the Performing Arts! I am thrilled to be here
with my wife, Chris, and from Atlanta, my sister-in-law Faye. And I
am especially pleased that, to help your ears recover from that poem,
we have some *real talent* this evening. Ready to entertain us are the
UF Concert Choir, Chamber Singers, Women's Chorale, Men's Glee

Club, Gainesville Civic Chorus, UF Symphony Orchestra and . . . last but not least . . . the Dance Theatre of Santa Fe College. I hope you enjoy the performance, and I wish all of you Happy Holidays and a Happy New Year!

5

Our Worthy Cause

In Celebration of Our New Cancer Hospital

*Remarks to major donors at a celebration of the opening of
the Shands at UF Cancer Hospital, October 15, 2009*

We welcome this addition to a health care system known for its quality, at a university devoted to research, in a state that would benefit from progress against cancer more than any other.

This in an era of great medical progress and even greater obstacles, in a time when we could decide whether it is possible to defeat the disease that has so often defeated us.

I could not be prouder that the University of Florida and Shands HealthCare are engaged in this epic struggle. We seek progress every day in our research labs, our pharmacies, and our surgical suites. And, with this new hospital, we bring those efforts to bear where it matters most, in the treatment and care of cancer patients.

We grasp the vastness of the challenge before us. That Florida, with its high elderly population, ranks second among the 50 states in number of cancer cases. That cancer will soon surpass heart disease, as well as AIDS, malaria, and tuberculosis combined, as the world's leading killer.

Yet, we gather hope from dispatches reporting progress, such as the recent announcement that UF scientists have found a gene therapy technique that seems to cut off the blood supply to tumors. We look forward to transforming this and other discoveries from UF's pioneering research into new treatments and cures for patients at this new hospital and everywhere.

Albert Schweitzer said, and I quote, "I have always held firmly to the thought that each one of us can do a little to bring some portion of misery to an end."

I celebrate each of you for your important contribution to this historic day. We will fight cancer *together*—at this hospital, at this university, and in classrooms and laboratories everywhere. And, with patience and focus, we will each do our part to bring some portion of the misery caused by cancer to an end.

In Recognition of Donors and Faculty

Remarks at the celebration of the success of the Florida Tomorrow capital campaign, October 5, 2012

This is quite a day! This morning, I joined 3,000 students and donors to celebrate all of the many student scholarships created in the campaign. Now, I have the privilege of honoring the donors who have been so supportive of our faculty. And, I also get to recognize the faculty members who are the reason for all the university's greatest achievements.

Many generous donors or their family members are here with us today. Also with us are many of the faculty whose research and scholarship is profoundly advanced by these endowments.

On each side are powerful stories. For donors, those stories may involve how they came to support a particular area of interest. For faculty, they may relate how these professors are making new discoveries and shedding new light on their fields.

I wish I could tell all of your stories. Since that is not possible, I will try to capture the academic dedication, and the generosity that enables it to flourish, through the stories of one donor and the faculty members whose work she supports . . . and how, together, they are changing lives to shape a more hopeful future for all of us.

I'll start with the donor, a UF alumna named Anita Zucker, who is represented here today by her sister-in-law, Mrs. Rochelle Marcus.

Mrs. Zucker's parents survived the Holocaust, and they taught her to treasure school and education. Perhaps that is why she majored in education at the University of Florida, graduating in 1972.

As her late husband, Jerry, also a 1972 UF graduate, built his business, Mrs. Zucker taught elementary school—beginning at two elementary schools just to the east in Putnam County, and later in South Carolina when the couple moved to Charleston.

She loved being a fourth- and fifth-grade teacher but was pained by the hardships of many of her students. More than three decades have passed, but she still remembers visiting homes with no floors, broken families, and children whose rage overshadowed all their other feelings.

She'll never forget one boy, Brent, at Lambs Elementary School in Charleston. As she tried to get him to focus on his work, Brent became infuriated and punched his hand through a classroom window.

Anita's husband was a phenomenally successful businessman who died in 2008. She then took the reins as chief executive of the global companies they had built together, Hudson Bay and InterTech.

Her commitment to education is part of a larger philosophy shared by the couple. This philosophy traces its roots to third-century Rabbinic teachings. It is called "Tikkun olam." It means "Repair the World."

Tikkun olam. "Repair the World." I can think of no better refrain for the works of the donors and faculty in this room today in the spirit of *Florida Tomorrow*.

Anita Zucker became a champion of education, and in 2011 she created the Anita Zucker Endowed Professorship in Early Childhood Studies as part of the *Florida Tomorrow* campaign here at her alma mater.

That brings me to the faculty part of my story.

Of all the problems that UF scientists and scholars are trying to solve, one of the most urgent problems involves helping our society do a better job of meeting the basic needs of our young children.

The statistics are daunting. A third of the nation's kids enter school unprepared. More than half cannot read at grade level by fourth grade.

These children often have mental, physical, or emotional challenges, and everyone recognizes that the best solution is to reach them before they reach school age. But we haven't figured out how to make that happen in their world—one with few quality child care options and too many impoverished and stressed families.

At UF, the Zucker professorship is empowering our faculty to find the answers.

The professorship supports the Center for Excellence in Early Childhood Studies in our College of Education. The center was founded just two years ago, but it has already won millions of dollars in federal grants to tackle every aspect of early childhood intervention . . . from basic research on the best tools and techniques . . . to hands-on assistance to teachers and caregivers.

The Center director, Dr. Patricia Snyder, is a pioneer who has experienced noted success in many aspects of early childhood education.

Dr. Snyder collaborates with UF colleagues from education, law, medicine, and other areas on research projects involving preschool teachers, caregivers, and parents. That "scholarship of engagement" is expected to directly impact the lives of 30,000 children over the next three years.

Tikkun olam. "Repair the World."

Within the *Florida Tomorrow* Campaign, there are dozens of donors with stories just as heartfelt as that of Mrs. Zucker—supporting dozens of faculty members who are just as committed to success as are the faculty in the Center for Excellence in Early Childhood Studies.

Their areas of inquiry range from improving surgical oncology . . . to exploring Jewish culture and society . . . to finding new ways to control agricultural pests . . . to creating new gene therapies . . . to unlocking the secrets of Asian art. Of course, these endowed professorships are created in perpetuity, which means this vital research is completely protected from the political and financial vagaries of state and federal budgets.

Donors, because of you, our faculty are changing the world . . . one medical breakthrough at a time . . . one archaeological find at a time . . . and one child at a time.

Speaking of which . . . let me conclude by telling you what happened to Brent, Mrs. Zucker's student in Charleston who put his hand through the window.

Brent went on to be a successful student, graduate from college . . . and today, he is a teacher himself. Mrs. Zucker ran into him recently, and he told her that she was the reason he chose the teaching profession. And now, they are friends . . . on Facebook!

The power of your donations means such stories will be multiplied by the hundreds across disciplines.

To the faculty here today, thank you for dreaming big about the difference that you can make in the world.

To the donors, thank you for investing in those dreams. Because of you, these faculty and the University of Florida are making them come true. Tikkun olam! "Repair the World."

Of Buildings and Blueberries

Remarks at the dedication of the Straughn Extension
Professional Development Center, January 12, 2012

What a smart meeting space you've created here! I share your enthusiasm that cooperative extension agents finally have a building all their own, their first on the University of Florida's main campus. Like all the best buildings, this one also speaks to a higher purpose—one powerfully conveyed by the unique medallion outside, above the front entrance.

What struck me about it was, it does not depict oranges or some other iconic Florida fruit. Rather, it depicts—unmistakably and forever—blueberries.

The medallion was inspired by Alto Straughn, whose generosity made this building possible. Mr. Straughn worked closely with the Institute of Food and Agricultural Sciences to develop, nurture, and promote blueberry plants that thrive amid Florida's climate and soil.

Thanks to his collaborations with IFAS extension, Florida blueberries have burst from hobby to crop. Mr. Straughn's success as Florida's largest blueberry grower is a big reason the state's blueberry production has soared tenfold over the past decade, to $65 million annually.

Our friends in the north have long relished winter citrus . . . from Florida. Today, in the spring, they gobble blueberries . . . from Florida. How tasty is that? In case you're wondering, this happy change also explains the blue wall in the lobby!

A thriving blueberry crop is new to the Sunshine State. But the mutually beneficial relationship between IFAS extension agents and Florida growers, ranchers, and farmers is long and enduring, and is the important relationship in Florida's $100 billion agriculture industry.

This space helps our extension agents stay abreast of the newest UF research and most pressing needs of our farmers. It provides a beautiful new headquarters for Florida 4-H. And it creates meeting and conference space for Florida agricultural groups.

Florida blueberries will bloom soon. Just as we look forward to the spring crop, we anticipate much more fruitful work between the University of Florida, IFAS extension, and Florida agriculture— aided by this vital new home.

Of Donors and Dreams

Remarks at the Deans Fundraising Workshop,
May 20, 2008

Since we are devoting this day to fundraising, I thought I would start with some facts about people with money.

Nearly 10 million Americans have a net worth of at least $1 million, a figure that excludes their primary residence. About 500,000 are worth more than $10 million.

Households with $25 million or more—there are an amazing 100,000 of those in this country. This spring, for the first time ever, the number of billionaires on the Forbes list cracked four figures, at 1,125. More than a third are Americans.

There is no shortage of potential big donors. In fact, there is an abundance. We *are*, however, experiencing a shortage—a shortage of grand ideas.

When it comes to seeking the generosity of the wealthiest people in this country and on this planet, we, at the University of Florida and other universities in this country . . . we are in need of more *dreams.* Projects so ambitious or unconventional that they capture the imaginations of the most sought-after donors.

We believe you, our top leaders, are in the best position to conceive these projects, to dream the dreams that resonate with these donors. This is why we brought you together for this workshop today.

Let me back up just a little.

We have raised over $650 million toward the *Florida Tomorrow* capital campaign's goal of $1.5 billion. Many of our contributions fall into the category of quote-unquote "loyalty gifts"—gifts from alumni or friends that arise out of allegiance to UF or to a UF college. While we value these gifts, we will never reach our goal on their strength alone.

The world's biggest donors today are not loyalty donors. They are transformational donors. They want to remake an institution, achieve a difficult goal, or be part of something risky, radical, or revolutionary.

We think we have the ingredients to make that possible at the University of Florida. But to do that, we will all have to change our traditional way of thinking.

If I asked each of you today what you would do with a wonderfully generous donation, you might say you would hire more faculty, create endowed chairs or, add scholarships. All of that is terrific and much needed.

But, these items are another set of bullets on another list of strategic objectives. They are not dreams.

Moreover, while you may wish to enhance your college or department, the transformational donor does not necessarily share your wishes. Research shows that people want to give philanthropically to satisfy different, even disparate, passions. Our job is to find ways for donors to fulfill these passions, and that will entail sharing donors across colleges, schools, and departments.

The phrase "that's my donor" may be the single biggest impediment we face in bringing in the largest gifts. Transformational donors want to put money toward a cause, not a kingdom.

So, as with many real dreams, yours should fly beyond your office, past your familiar hallways, through the walls of this university. With the donor's help, you may do the work in many different divisions or departments at this university.

But your goal is broader still: you have a vision for making the world better in some substantial way.

I want to give you a couple of examples of the kind of dream and donor we're seeking.

Three years ago, Tufts University in Massachusetts received a $100 million donation, its largest gift ever, from Pierre Omidyar, the founder of eBay.

Omidyar and his wife, Pam, worked out an agreement with Tufts whereby the university would use the money to make microloans in developing countries. The returns support Tufts' financial aid programs and scholarships and are reinvested to support more microloans.

The Omidyars are Tufts alumni, which undoubtedly played a role in their generosity. But, had Tufts not been open to this radical idea of growing a university endowment via a social good, it's a fair bet the eBay founder would have taken his donation elsewhere.

We have examples of transformational gifts on our own campus as well. Thanks to William and Evelyn McKnight, we created something that had never existed at UF before and remains rare on other campuses today—the multidisciplinary Brain Institute.

Thanks to Jim and Alexis Pugh, we built Pugh Hall, a building that, very much by design, houses the path-breaking Bob Graham Center for Public Service.

In 2006, a St. Petersburg heart surgeon, Crayton Pruitt, transformed UF's then-tiny biomedical engineering department into a thriving and growing one. Dean Khargonekar will discuss this gift later today, and I don't want to spoil his presentation, but there's no question Dr. Pruitt's grand ambitions cried out for an appropriately grand response.

Ambitions. Dreams. Transformations. Given the painful budget cuts you are all experiencing, it may seem utterly the wrong moment to ask for your leadership in this important cause. You might also think that you have enough to worry about, that this is a job for the professionals in development.

But, I would make just the contrary arguments. We should dream our greatest dreams in our most distressing times. And you, the academic leaders of this university, are those most capable of conceiving and articulating the dreams we seek. Even if this activity doesn't lead to a major gift or gifts, it will remind us of our largest and most noble goals as scholars and scientists.

I started with some facts about money, and I would like to end with facts about money.

To reach the *Florida Tomorrow* goal of $1.5 billion, our development folks believe we need at least one $100 million gift, one $75 million gift, and two $50 million gifts. We also need many more $25 million, $10 million, and $5 million gifts.

We may well attract some of these gifts in the traditional ways. But, I firmly believe that, with the help of your valued guidance and expert assistance, we will draw the attention of our most outsized donors with our most outsized dreams.

6

Joining Discovery
to Technology

A Building and an Idea

*Remarks at the opening ceremonies for the Florida
Innovation Hub, January 11, 2012*

In an institution as old as the University of Florida, it is rare to experience an occasion that feels historic. This dedication is one of those rare occasions. That's because the Innovation Hub is the "cornerstone of a landmark."

Innovation Hub, as both the building itself and the idea behind it, is the "cornerstone of a landmark" for the university . . . for this community . . . for the state of Florida . . . and most of all, for the innovative things we will do to better human lives.

From at least the time of the Old Testament, a cornerstone has represented both a unifying foundation in architecture—and a fundamentally important idea. For a building, the cornerstone sets the pattern of every other stone that's laid. As a foundational idea, the cornerstone sets the tone, pointing everyone toward a higher, better goal.

The Innovation Hub cornerstone has four sides. The first is the final fusion of UF entrepreneurship with UF research.

This side began half a century ago with a certain yellow concoction invented by Dr. Robert Cade and continued with the opening in 1995 of our biotechnology incubator in Alachua. And, it flourishes today with a steady stream of UF patents and licenses, and with successful companies such as RTI Biologics, Xhale Innovations, and Sinmat.

The Hub finally gathers under one roof venture capitalists, product designers, accountants, intellectual property law firms, and our technology licensing experts—in a space meticulously designed to nurture their creativity. And the Hub finally gives us a place where a mere five-minute walk separates our visionary faculty from the professionals who make their ideas real.

The second side in the Innovation Hub cornerstone is a new, seamless Gainesville—a Gainesville where one cannot know where the university ends and the community begins.

It was not so long ago that UF and the City of Gainesville went about their business separately, if not in opposition. Their separation set the tone for a community divided over how to grow and prosper. Not surprisingly, the city's geography arranged itself in mirror image of this division.

How things have changed. Today, we have a shared faith in the power of innovation to bring economic prosperity while preserving Gainesville's distinctive quality of life. The Florida Innovation Hub is the first building in the partnership called Innovation Square that will close the last remaining physical gap between town and gown.

An empty 40 acres will be filled. Spatially, with technology start-ups, apartments, restaurants, galleries, and local retail outlets. And metaphorically, with a culture that draws together artists and innovators with the human characteristic that unites them both: creativity.

The third side of the Innovation Hub cornerstone involves the state: it is the increased influence of UF innovation on the jobs, opportunities, and life experience all Floridians deserve—one that should be every bit as bright and sustaining as the sun and surf that lured so many here.

UF and its spinoffs already contribute to Florida's high-tech industry, recognized not only for rapid growth, but also for high salaries and family-friendly workplaces.

Our biggest spinoff employs more than 700 men and women. Our startups together generate 8,000 jobs statewide, giving Florida the building blocks for a more diverse and resilient economy in the 21st century.

To add to these opportunities, we must create more new businesses and the Hub answers this call. This incubator began accepting tenants a mere three months ago. Already no fewer than 15 technology companies have set up shop.

Companies named One Software, Generation Wy, and Shadow Health—these are among the tenants that represent fifteen possibilities of companies that will someday build their own headquarters and employ their own staff of Floridians. And . . . surely on this day we can allow ourselves to dream a little . . . fifteen more chances at Florida's version of a blockbuster like those that originated at universities elsewhere—Google, Facebook, Dell.

The final foundation of this historic cornerstone is the one that matters most. It is the enhanced potential for human good, from Gainesville to the world.

Glaucoma sufferers who've realized improved vision thanks to Trusopt, UF's glaucoma drug, understand that this potential is very real. Homeowners who have kept houses safe with Sentricon, the university's anti-termite system, know it too. So also our state realizes the benefit.

This month, we launch Florida's first industrial-scale production plant for a sustainable biofuel in Perry, Florida. That plant is made possible thanks only to a UF technology.

The Hub will build up UF, Gainesville, and Florida, but its real meaning is the greater opportunity to change life for the better. Even if this is a long way off, we gain the faith today that we can be part of something greater than ourselves.

Many of you in the audience have worked tirelessly to promote UF innovation, smart urban growth, and the local creative economy since long before we even had names for those things. I applaud each of you for your foresight and perseverance.

Whether you have worked toward this day for years, or you are new to Gainesville and the Florida Innovation Hub, you are now part of the mortar that will build this cornerstone to its full potential. I wish you well as you work to make Innovation Hub—the building and the idea—a historic landmark for our campus, our community, our state, and our human future.

A New Frontier in Orlando

Remarks at the dedication for the UF Research and
Academic Center at Lake Nona, November 20, 2012

As we all know from science, a change in "a paradigm shift" can sometimes result in a quantum leap forward. That is the guiding principle behind this beautiful building we are gathered today to celebrate. It is the guiding principle behind Medical City. And, it is the trajectory of the next chapter in the story of Orlando—and indeed, in the story of the state of Florida.

The University of Florida has built nearly 1,000 buildings in the 106 years since we opened in Gainesville, almost all of them on our main campus. We also reach out with agricultural facilities in all of Florida's 67 counties, including meaningful citrus research here in Central Florida. This is our mission as a land-grant university.

Now, as the nation celebrates the 150th anniversary of the Morrill Act that established the land-grants, we are taking that mission in an entirely new direction—the most visible example of which is right here, with UF's first medical-research building outside our historic home.

With this significant investment of research funding and people here at Lake Nona, 112 miles from Gainesville, we join the Sanford-Burnham Medical Research Institute and the other institutions at Medical City in another departure from tradition.

We alter our historic trajectories as proudly independent institutions. We chart a new path as partners.

Each of these partners seeks to translate discoveries into products that help people. Each seeks to accelerate the growth of Florida's biotechnology economy and its high-skill, high-wage jobs. With this new building, and with Medical City, we commit to a new future of achieving those goals, not separately as we have in the past, but together.

The vision of an international hub for biotechnology and the life sciences is, of course, a break with the tradition of Florida as the nation's vacation destination. But, let us remember that tradition, too, is rooted in a new direction—one that began right here in Orlando.

Forty-seven years ago this month, dignitaries from around the state gathered in this city for another historic launch. Florida governor Haydon Burns began the press conference, then turned the microphone over to the man everyone wanted to hear from. That man was Walt Disney, who was in town to announce a project he called Disney World.

Walt Disney stressed that though Disney World might share some traits with the older Disneyland in California, it would be its own, utterly unique, Florida creation.

He said, and I quote, "I want life to create new things. You hate to repeat yourself. I don't like to make sequels to my pictures. I like to take a new thing and develop a new concept."

Not a repeat. A new thing. A new concept. No better words capture the spirit of our gathering today.

In the same way Disney World helped shape the Orlando and Florida of the 20th century, so this new building and Medical City will shape the Orlando and Florida of the 21st century—and the University of Florida looks forward to working with all of you as we make this quantum leap forward.

A New "Mental Giant"

Remarks at the opening of the UF Data Center, May 7, 2013

We get to mark two milestones today: the public debut of the university's new supercomputer, "HiPerGator," which occupies one half of the Data Center, and the launch of a new centralized computing facility for university operations in the other half.

I'd like to recognize these milestones one at a time, starting with HiPerGator.

To help us appreciate the leap forward we make today, I want to take a step back ... *way* back ... to the university's first foray into the brave new world of computing.

That was in 1956, when we purchased one of the early mainframes, an IBM 650. The computer could perform 100 multiplications per second, a speed considered *so* fast that a university press release described the 650 as ... quote ... "a mental giant of the Atomic Age."

Fifty-seven years later, HiPerGator operates at speeds of 150 *trillion* multiplications per second.

Built by Dell, it is the most powerful supercomputer in the state of Florida. Connected to UF's 100-gigabit Internet pipeline, it is truly a scientific resource for the globe.

As a result, just as the university's "mental giant" helped us explore cutting-edge science a half-century ago, so HiPerGator makes possible profound new research for *our time*.

We see this in the physics research to be conducted with HiPerGator.

As many of you will recall, physicists at the particle collider near Geneva announced last summer they had detected signs of a particle that could be the elusive Higgs Boson, a.k.a. "the God Particle." UF had one of the largest teams of physicists working at the collider at CERN.

Evidence is not proof. To confirm the Higgs, research teams around the globe have to sort out the products of the high-energy collisions using *huge* numbers of calculations. HiPerGator is a hub for this key activity.

In other words, with the assistance of HiPerGator, we will seek to complete the last piece of the puzzle about the structure of our universe. This is an effort to solve a scientific puzzle not just of *our time*, but of *all time*.

Other UF researchers will use HiPerGator to pursue similarly *foundational* and *far-reaching* research, from filling in the branches of the evolutionary tree of life to identifying the genetic roots of disease. In fact, dozens of groups from a diversity of disciplines will tap the supercomputer's powers—keeping it every bit as busy as its neighbor across the hall.

That brings me to the other half of the UF Data Center, the half devoted to university operations.

Just as HiPerGator represents a foundational and far-reaching step for research, so the other part of the building represents a foundational and far-reaching step for university operations.

This is true for two reasons.

First, the facility brings together from across campus all the computing power needed to run the university.

Maintaining student records . . . handling registration for classes . . . human resources . . . these and other activities now have a single, more efficient, and more reliable home.

As HiPerGator leverages scientists' abilities to make new discoveries, so this facility helps our professionals and faculty advance the university—from grant-writing to grading.

Second, the UF Data Center is secure, with carefully thought-out safeguards to ensure continuation of services under any conditions.

Chief Operating Officer Win Phillips will describe some of these measures in a moment. Suffice it to say, this center is designed to protect the university's information heartbeat from threats, both natural and manmade.

As I wrap up, I want to note that the Data Center was completed *under budget* and *on schedule*. This is a tribute to Elias Eldayrie's leadership and the work of many, many others in Information Technology—as well as the assistance and cooperation of an incredibly diverse collection of faculty and administrators.

This is a big deal for UF!

Hearkening to our missions as a public university, we give students the STEM skills in such great demand by employers. We provide a service to all those worldwide who want to tap the potential of "Big Data." And we plant the seeds for the new technologies and spinoff companies that are making innovation and entrepreneurship a mainstay of our campus and community.

Just as was the case with that IBM 650 more than a half-century ago, these are goals that demand our attention in *our time* and for *all time.*

Bringing Science to the Public Square

Remarks to the National Association of Science Writers at the opening reception of the association's annual meeting, November 1, 2013

I know some of you toured our natural history and butterfly museums earlier, and I believe you'll have the chance to visit our premier research and tech-transfer facilities. Some of you will even plunge into the crystal springs that distinguish this part of Florida—be warned, they're cold!

You've truly come to an incredible university and region. But since you're journalists, I know you'll also figure out some of our shortcomings. So, I thought you might appreciate it if I saved you the trouble.

As you may have read, Gainesville is in fact the former home of Terry Jones, the preacher who thought it was a good idea to burn Korans. And yes, our district elected the Tea Party congressman who claimed defaulting on the federal debt would enhance world fiscal stability.

And about those springs: we even have some residents who believe they're turning cloudy not because of human or agricultural runoff, but because of manatee poop!

It's funny, but it points to a larger problem of public ignorance and rejection of science. This is a worrisome issue, and one that underscores your importance as science writers.

We know our springs here in Florida are losing their clarity because of nutrient pollution. But the example of ignorance and rejection of science that touches us wherever we live is climate change.

I am sure you joined me in noting the silence surrounding the U.N. climate panel's report on climate change a month ago. That silence was especially galling in Florida, where 2.4 million residents live less than four feet above sea level.

I was one of 12 founding signatory presidents on the American College and University President's Climate Commitment. I'm proud that UF is home to hundreds of scholars working on various aspects of climate change—some of whom you'll hear from during this conference.

The science is strong. The problem is the disconnect among the scientists, public-policy makers, and citizens themselves.

Our salvation surely rests with you and with your role in bringing science to the public square—and helping to banish the non-science already there.

What's true of the Florida springs and climate change is also true of declining freshwater, clean energy production, growing enough food to feed seven billion people . . . and so many other challenges.

Science is far from perfect, but it's all we have. When you shine a light on scientists and their work, revealing both the strengths and the flaws, you beat back the darkness and denial that offer no future.

All of which brings me back to ScienceWriters13 and your next four days at UF.

We have some of our best faculty on hand to share their exciting work. We're proud to show you some of our most unique research initiatives. I know you'll make the most of these opportunities to learn and discover.

But I also hope you'll find some time to enjoy yourselves and soak up some of the inspiration that all writers need to remain fresh and creative. Whether you discover it visiting beautiful butterflies next door, or during a plunge into a magical spring next Tuesday, let this conference recharge you.

Because both our scientists and our public need you; you have some very important work ahead!

A Shared Voyage of Discovery

Remarks celebrating UF's partnership in the world's
largest optical telescope, Coral Gables,
June 29, 2006

This reception occurs on a historic date. Eleven years ago today, on June 29, 1995, the Space Shuttle *Atlantis* docked with the Russian Mir space station. It was the shuttle's first docking mission in the first phase of the International Space Station.

Nations have a long tradition of coming together on great voyages of exploration and discovery. Tonight, we are gathered here to celebrate another historic transnational partnership in discovery—the Gran Telescopio Canarias.

The University of Florida, and public institutions in Spain and Mexico, have joined hands to build the GTC. The silver-domed telescope will be the largest optical telescope in the world upon its completion late next year.

As we have just seen in the video, the GTC's remarkable 34.1-foot mirror will allow it to collect light from the faintest and most distant objects in the universe. That light will contain tell-tale evidence of new planets, ancient galaxies, and emerging stars.

To make sense of that evidence, the GTC will rely on highly sophisticated, complex instruments. I am proud that UF is building one of the first such instruments to be available for permanent use on the telescope, an infrared camera and spectrograph called CanariCam.

I am equally pleased that UF's instrument builders are working with counterparts in Spain and Mexico on other innovative instruments for the GTC.

Indeed, our partnership with our friends in Spain and Mexico was never, for the University of Florida, simply a matter of securing observation time on the world's best telescope.

We are supporting graduate and postdoctoral students from Spain. We are encouraging faculty exchanges between our three countries.

This is not just a global facility. It is a global research effort.

That also describes the International Space Station—where, by the way, the shuttle *Discovery* is headed after it blasts off on Saturday.

These collaborations have huge benefits for their participants. Just as the Russian and American space programs helped loft these countries to technological and scientific prominence, so the GTC will propel its partners into the top ranks of the world's astronomers.

I am excited about the result, both in terms of the discoveries to be made and their positive influence on the member institutions. I wish everyone here the greatest success in this important endeavor.

Building Collaboration

Remarks at the dedication of the Biomedical Sciences
Building, May 11, 2010

I came here from a luncheon honoring donors who were key to making this building possible. One of those donors is a St. Petersburg cardiothoracic surgeon, J. Crayton Pruitt.

Fifteen years ago, Dr. Pruitt's heart was failing, and he was admitted to Shands for a heart transplant. There was no donor heart available, so until one arrived Dr. Pruitt was assisted by a machine called a biventricular assist device.

After a successful heart transplant Dr. Pruitt is still with us and has had many productive years. This experience led Dr. Pruitt and his family to donate $10 million to the University of Florida to start UF's biomedical engineering department.

Medicine today relies on an alliance between human and machine, doctors and engineers, scientists, scholars, therapists, and experts from other fields.

The collaborative research that underpins this alliance is the heart of this new building. Increasingly, it is also the heart of the University of Florida.

This is demonstrated by this building's location, literally bridging medicine, engineering, and public health.

The geography makes it a snap for biomedical engineers to work with neuroscientists based in the McKnight Brain Institute, and scientists and biomedical engineers need only take a short walk to have lunch with clinicians at Shands.

Within this building, there is a rich assortment of units from three colleges: Biomedical Engineering, the Howard Hughes Medical Institute Undergraduate Research Laboratory, the Diabetes Center of Excellence, the Center for Translational Research in Neurodegenerative Diseases, and researchers from the Department of Physical Therapy.

The architect Frank Lloyd Wright said, "The space within becomes the reality of the building."

Everything about the Biomedical Sciences Building's interior design bends toward researchers working together.

Laboratories are separated into bays rather than walled off into rooms to encourage students and faculty to mingle. People can also meet in this stunning atrium, named the Broad-Bussel Atrium in honor of the donor, the Shepard Broad Foundation. Both the layout of the labs and the atrium recognize that good science often originates in a chance encounter.

The Biomedical Sciences Building embodies a transformation happening across the University of Florida.

It arrives on the heels of the Cancer and Genetics Research Complex, the Nanoscale Research Facility, and the Emerging Pathogens Institute, all of which also make research collaboration a central design theme.

A fourth such building, the Institute on Aging Clinical Translational Research Building, is in the planning stages. As the academic walls between disciplines fall, so will the brick and mortar ones.

All of this is critical for research progress, but what counts is whether it will make people's lives better. The evidence suggests it will.

Epilepsy patients stand to benefit from research aimed at interrupting seizures. Diabetes sufferers could see new treatments as a result of pioneering work by biomedical engineers and diabetes researchers here.

We are literally stitching collaboration into the culture: the express goal of the HHMI Undergraduate Research Laboratory is to inculcate collaboration into the next generation of scientists.

This building has only been occupied a few months, but it is already proving its worth.

Up on the third floor, a biomedical engineer has an office just a couple of doors down from an assistant professor of physical therapy.

Peter McFetridge and Andy Judge ran into each other in the hall a few times and got to talking. They learned both do research related to human tissue. Peter works on tissue engineering, Andy on muscle atrophy, but they liked each other's company, and their conversations revealed they shared common interests.

Used to be, all of the faculty members in the Department of Physical Therapy were in the Health Professions/Nursing/Pharmacy Complex.

Biomedical engineering was divided up among three buildings. There was little chance faculty would run into each other.

Academically, biomedical engineering and physical therapy are pretty far apart, and a meeting of the minds is unlikely. Even if researchers were to cross paths, they would have no way to see if they liked each other—and as we all know, it's really important to like the person you're trying to collaborate with!

In short, Peter, the biomedical engineer, and Andy, the physical therapy researcher, probably would have remained strangers. Instead, they have gotten to know each other well enough to discuss a joint project, and they may pool their resources to buy a piece of equipment they both need. Peter said, and I quote, "I've got a good feeling something will come out of it."

So do I!

Geographically and philosophically, this building is the heart of University of Florida research as it stands today. We all look forward to the collaborations among engineering, medical, and public health researchers here—and to the life-giving treatments and cures that result.

Grow the Little Fish

Remarks at the Southern Governors' Association Annual
Meeting, Asheville, North Carolina, August 20, 2011

As a member of Governor Rick Scott's Economic Development Transition Team, I have firsthand appreciation for his commitment to economic development and job growth in Florida. I am sure that each of you share that commitment on behalf of your own states.

We know that enticing auto factories or research institutes can have long-term payoffs. We also know those deals are costly—and that at this moment, corporations and institutes are hoarding their cash rather than expanding.

Meanwhile, states are in no position to pump taxpayer dollars into generous incentives to attract the biggest fish in the sea.

But now is an excellent time to invest in startups spawned by universities. Researchers have found that when the NASDAQ dives, the number of university startups soar, because investors have fewer places to put their money. Nationally, universities already spin off about 600 startups every year, and nearly three-quarters remain in the states where they are started.

No doubt, we all love to hook big fish. But the better option today is to stock your pond with little fish that could grow into lunkers. The University of Florida, and the research universities in your own states, want to help.

We want to hatch the little fish, the startups that become major employers, economic drivers, and tax-revenue generators.

Most states have invested in the innovation economy, though their tactics vary. Last decade, Florida went fishing for whoppers. In 2004, the state spent $310 million to lure the Scripps Research Institute, with local governments kicking in $269 million. In 2006, lawmakers spent $450 million more to lure seven major research institutes.

Everyone agrees that the return on these sorts of investments can take decades, and Florida's experience proves that rule. The Scripps Florida campus now employs a total of about 450 staff members, which so far works out to over $1 million per job.

Meanwhile, state policy analysts last year urged shifting state investment from "attracting new research institutes to providing early stage capital for startup biotechnology companies."

In other words, grow the little fish. That is exactly the strategy being embraced by Texas, home to at least 30 percent of the nation's new net jobs in the past two years. Since 2005, the Lone Star State's Emerging Technology Fund has sent nearly $200 million to 133 early stage companies that collaborate with the state's universities.

In this economy, feeding those little fingerlings in what I might call the "innovation hatchery" is an excellent strategy for job growth. Let me explain how by turning to my own university.

UF is Florida's largest research university and one of the nation's most comprehensive, with 5,000 faculty and $678 million in annual research funding. But we were a sleepy southern land-grant university until one day in 1965, when . . . eureka! . . . one of our scientists had an idea.

Dr. Robert Cade, a UF nephrologist, mixed up a liquid concoction to give Gator football players an energy boost.

The players liked the energy but didn't care for the taste, so Dr. Cade's wife suggested he pour in some lemon juice. In 1967, Stokely–Van Camp began marketing the pale yellow mixture known by then as "Gatorade."

The sports drink industry was born, and UF had a new source of revenue to plow into research and innovation.

After the Bayh-Dole Act freed universities to profit from their inventions, UF transformed 200 acres into "Progress Park" for university technology spinoffs. In 1998, one of those spinoffs was a biotech company, RTI Biologics, that makes biological implants for surgeries. Today, RTI has 700 employees.

In other words, we've grown our own pretty big fish—in our own pond.

In 1995, UF, the state, and the federal government built one of the nation's first bio-business incubators. So far, that incubator has nurtured 41 companies that have created about 750 jobs. It now has a $100 million annual economic impact in our home county.

We built this small incubator for only $11.5 million. And remember, biotech jobs are high-wage, high-skill jobs, with Florida biotech workers earning nearly 40 percent more than the state's average workers.

In the past decade, we have focused on new sources of investment, especially the private sector, because we don't want to depend on increasingly scarce state funds.

These investments have had a big impact. Today, UF patents about 150 inventions and spins off about a dozen companies each year.

And, we have passed what seems to be the ultimate litmus test for technology communities. Facebook founder Mark Zuckerberg dropped out of Harvard. Apple founder Steve Jobs dropped out of Reed. And, now one of Gainesville's hottest startups, a music-sharing company called Grooveshark with 80 employees, was co-founded by Josh Greenberg . . . yes . . . a UF dropout.

Most UF startups remain small, and, like all startups, they face a sea of hazards ... from the struggle for funding ... to aggressive competitors ... to surviving in an unforgiving economy.

But states and universities can work together in partnership to develop and grow these startups.

Our partnership begins with state support for university research. State dollars helped pay for four new UF research buildings. Since the first was completed in 2006, these buildings have supported $166 million in sponsored research. Of course, states also help startups through investing in research. Last year, the state of Florida provided nearly $61 million in contracts and grants to our faculty.

States can also invest in university startups directly. UF advised lawmakers on a 2007 law that enabled the Florida Retirement System's pension fund to devote 1.5 percent of its assets to Florida-centric technology and growth investments. The Florida Growth Fund's investments in Florida companies will soon total $500 million.

Startups often have a tough time bridging government research funding and venture investment. State support at this stage can be a lifesaver. Florida lends a hand through the Florida Opportunity Fund, which invests in venture capital firms committed to financing seed and early stage companies. This spring, the state also dedicated $10 million for seed grants for Florida startups.

There are many, many more creative possibilities for state-university partnerships. But in the end, what matters most is what we do for creative *people*. California has this one figured out, but don't think for a moment that the Golden State has a monopoly.

So let me conclude with a question: How can we discover, attract and nurture the *people* who will become the South's next technology icons?

7

Building Bridges,
Bridging Differences

A Dwelling Place for Goodness

*Remarks at the groundbreaking for the Lubavitch-Chabad
Center for Jewish Life and Learning,
March 25, 2012*

Rabbi Goldman, two years ago, at the 10th anniversary celebration
of the Lubavitch-Chabad Jewish Student Center, you and Chanie
gave Chris and me a beautiful wall plaque—a Blessing for the Home
in the Jewish tradition. We proudly hung it in a prominent spot in
our house, and it has brought us many compliments. And, I believe,
many blessings on our home.

You have made us feel warm and happy in our home, and I am
so pleased today to also give you a gift as you build your home. The
inscription reads, "May your walls know joy, serenity and love."

I want to give you this plaque to remember this special day. It is
truly special for me, as well, because it is my eldest son's birthday.

Welcome, everyone, to this groundbreaking for the new Center for Jewish Life and Learning. After 12 years in Gainesville . . . some portions of which were spent in a tent . . . I sense among everyone here today an overwhelming feeling of joy.

A lot of people came together for this memorable moment. Let me recognize Moshe and Lillian Tabacinic for their extraordinary generosity in helping to make this center possible. I would also like to single out Mary and Roy Paulson, neighbors who have been unwavering friends and supporters to the Goldmans and the Center.

We at the University of Florida deeply value the diversity of faiths that are such a part of the fabric of our university community. Religious organizations with ties to campus enrich our discourse and enliven our spirit, and they are at our side in moments of celebration and times of crisis.

They are also a source of strength and comfort to our students—and that is why I am so pleased to join you today to mark the construction of the Center for Jewish Life and Learning.

Students arrive at our doorstep bright, accomplished . . . and also young, inexperienced, and often away from home for the first time. It is neither unexpected nor unusual for them to experience personal or academic trials in their journey through college.

Our academic counselors and staff at the Counseling and Wellness Center are there to help students overcome these trials, but many students understandably need the comfort of their faiths.

You here at Lubavitch-Chabad have a strong tradition of welcoming UF's Jewish students in times of need, and also in joyous times. You are a home away from home . . . and when this building is completed, what a home you will have!

A synagogue, guest wing, library, fitness room, kosher café . . . and a parsonage for Rabbi Goldman and his family, allowing them to continue their tradition of extending their family's bonds to our family of Jewish students.

This Center for Jewish Life and Learning will be a safe haven, a place of refuge, and it will also be a gathering place for parents, alumni, and friends.

Your vision for this building harkens a section in the Torah where God commands the Jewish people to build a dwelling place for the tablets containing the Ten Commandments. God says of the tablets, "I will dwell within them."

This phrase suggests that every act of kindness, every good deed, every humane and generous action—all are dwelling places for God and His goodness.

I look forward to you completing this dwelling place, and to all the good it will do for students, for the University of Florida, and for the Gainesville community.

Bourbon Redeemers, Toledo Mud Hens, and the Tom Petty Tree

Remarks delivered to the Community Campus Council in the Reitz Union's Arredondo Room, September 13, 2006

I can't think of a better place to ponder the University of Florida's 100th anniversary in the City of Gainesville than here in the Arredondo Room. With the view from the balcony, you can really start to appreciate this flagship university and the town beyond.

It makes me wonder, what would the view be like from other places in Florida that wanted this university?

For example, that small town to the northeast of us . . . Fernandina Beach.

Perhaps you didn't know this little beach town near Jacksonville, famous for its shrimp, courted UF at the turn of the century. One Fernandina booster had a novel pitch. "If we once get the boys on the island," he said, "they can't run away from school without getting caught at the drawbridge."

If that argument had flown, the view from up here might have been shrimp boats and the Atlantic Ocean. And a heck of a lot of traffic at that drawbridge.

A small community near Melbourne, Eau Gallie, was a more serious contender for UF. There, during Reconstruction, a wealthy Wisconsin family donated 1,000 acres for the university. That acreage was along the banks of the Indian River, and workers even cleared it and started to build. So we might have had a riverfront view from up here . . . except Reconstruction ended and the old guard came back to power. That group, the Bourbon Redeemers—yes, that's actually what they were called—quickly nixed the Yankee land donation in Eau Gallie.

Most of you know the official story. Florida's first land-grant college, the Florida Agricultural College, opened in Lake City in 1884. That college became the University of Florida in 1903. Gainesville lobbied for and won the university in 1906.

When a telegraph office in Gainesville announced the news to the waiting crowd, the celebration included church bells, a parade, and firecrackers. I won't claim the relationship between UF and the City of Gainesville has always been one of cheers and church bells. And I know the fireworks haven't always been the celebratory kind. But these two institutions certainly have contributed immensely to each other's growth and prosperity. We could not exist without one another.

Such a symbiotic town-gown relationship is worth celebrating, especially now, in the fall. Homecoming is less than a month away. On University Avenue, Gainesville's high school bands will join UF's marching band as city and university police keep the sirens blaring— to the delight of Alachua County's schoolchildren.

With that sense of celebration in mind, I'd like to tell some more tales about this campus and the town that it calls home.

. . .

First, in the spirit of the season, a word or two about athletics. You know all about football and basketball programs, but did you know the University of Florida and Gainesville attempted to get the New York Giants to use UF as its spring training facility? The Giants came here in 1919—but only, it must be remembered, after we agreed to install showers in the gym. The City of Gainesville paid for those showers. Alas, the Giants did not return in 1920.

UF was also the spring training site for another famous baseball team, the Toledo Mud Hens, who used our facilities in the 1950s. You may recall, the Mud Hens were the beloved team of Corporal Klinger in the show *M*A*S*H*.

If we never managed to hold on to a spring training team, our athletic program today is a huge reason for the university's success and a wonderful resource for this community.

. . .

I bet a lot of people in this room have tickets for the Tom Petty concert a week from tomorrow. It's Petty's first visit to his hometown in 13 years. Although Petty, a graduate of Gainesville High School, never attended UF, he did spend some time on our campus. He worked briefly on our grounds crew, planting trees.

Some senior employees in the physical plant still remember him. They affectionately call one of the trees he planted, an Ogeechee lime, the "Tom Petty Tree."

That lime is not the only tree on campus with a story to tell. There's a sycamore known as the moon tree because it grew out of a seed toted to the moon and back aboard Apollo 14. And although the big live oaks on campus seem the most ancient, our oldest trees are our towering longleaf pines. Some have passed their 200th birthdays! A lot of these old pines lean to the south. That's their way of telling you about a hurricane that blew through town several decades ago.

A recent survey revealed that we have 183 tree species on campus. How fitting for Gainesville, which in this growing state of 17 million people still deserves its appellation as "The Tree City. . . ."

We have a lot of trees, but our main job since the days of the Florida Agricultural College has been nurturing students. A lot of people think our first students mostly majored in agriculture. To the contrary, although we were called an agricultural college, the agricultural arts drew only a handful of students!

We have those Bourbon Redeemers to thank. They were anti-government types who didn't believe in public dollars to educate the common man. In fact, for many years, they even refused to provide state funding for their land-grant college!

According to university historian Carl Van Ness, arts and sciences had a much larger enrollment than agriculture. And when our law school opened in 1909, it quickly began graduating more students than any other.

Alachua County was essential to our early success in Gainesville—the county consistently contributed more students to UF than any other county through 1938. That said, attrition in the early years was horrendous. Until the early 1930s, about one-third of the students in our freshman and sophomore classes withdrew every year due to poverty and poor preparation.

Alumni from that era remember doom-and-gloom speeches to freshmen. "Look to your left and right," they were told. "Only one of the three of you will receive a diploma."

Today, our freshman attrition rate is well under 10 percent. Our agriculture program is strong, but the College of Liberal Arts and Sciences remains the most popular home for undergraduates, with 13,000 majors this school year. Careers in health completely dominate students' ambitions. Fully one-third of the students who come to UF today describe themselves as pre-health majors.

Are students looking at the aging population and making informed decisions about their career paths? Well . . . maybe. Actually, television plays a powerful role in these kinds of enrollment trends. *CSI Miami* has spurred a huge interest in criminology and forensic pathology. Ditto *Grey's Anatomy* for medicine. When *LA Law* was the hot show on the tube, pre-law majors.

No word yet on the impact *Desperate Housewives* will have!

The demographics make us confident that students who graduate with health-related degrees will steer themselves into well-paying, productive careers. That's in many ways the point of what we do—create an educated workforce that meets our society's needs.

We are also a research institution. You've probably already heard that our scientists and engineers passed the half billion mark in research dollars this year.

Here's something you haven't heard. Doug Jones, director of the Florida Museum of Natural History, tells me that William and Nadine McGuire, patrons of the McGuire Center for Lepidoptera and Biodiversity, have just donated a new collection of 2.5 million specimens. That will bring UF's collection of butterflies and moths to 8.5 million, about 100,000 specimens more than London's Natural History Museum. As a result, UF now has the world's largest butterfly collection!

Not all of the museum's 20-million-plus specimens are as charismatic or colorful as butterflies. There's the blue-green algae fossils, for example. These are some of the earliest fossils on earth, dating back 3.5 billion years. Think of it—3.5 billion-year-old algae. No wonder it's so hard to get that stuff out of the pool!

From modern times, the museum houses many significant artifacts from St. Augustine, Florida's and the nation's first city. These include Spanish gold from some of the first Europeans to reach our shores.

The Florida Museum of Natural History is an archive of life. It is also a preserver of our state and local heritage. University and community are much enriched as a result.

. . .

I mentioned the $518.8 million we received in research funding this year. Here's another number for you: 4,344,850. No, that's not the total of parking tickets UPD doles out each year. It's the number of trash bags we used on campus last year. Truly. And those four-million-plus trash bags weighed 163 tons . . . without the trash!

I gleaned this smelly little factoid from internal research tied to our sustainability initiative, the University of Florida's ongoing effort to go green. We need this kind of detail to figure out how we can reach our goals. In the case of trash, we've pledged to try to reduce our solid waste to zero by 2015. You can see what an enormous job we've created for ourselves from that trash bag figure alone.

Last year UF bought 416,000 megawatt hours of electricity, enough for about 46,000 homes. Our projected power bill this year is $15 million—double that for all our utilities. So building energy-efficient buildings and our other environmentally friendly initiatives are also smart economics for us.

Gainesville and Alachua County have a long history as environmentally minded communities. A few years ago, Alachua County voters approved a property tax increase to fund $29 million for the land conservation program, Alachua County Forever. UF's sustainability initiative dovetails with this local green ethic.

. . .

On the year of our 100th anniversary in Gainesville, a natural question is, "what does the future hold?"

I mentioned our students' interest in health careers, and I think that gives us a clue. More than $250 million, or the majority of UF's research funding today, supports research in the biological sciences. The just-completed Cancer and Genetics Research Building, the biggest research building on campus, is devoted to biological sciences— as are the pending Biomedical Science Building and Pathogen Research Facility.

The point is, we're striving to establish ourselves as leaders in what J. Craig Venter, the pioneer in gene sequencing, calls the "century of biology." If we can do that—and I believe we can—it will be a good thing for UF, Gainesville, and Florida.

What are random facts to some people are passions to others. For the sports fans in the audience, I hope you were glad to learn that the Toledo Mud Hens once hit a few balls from our campus. Music fans, if you want to check out that Tom Petty lime tree, it's near Phelps Lab close to the Reitz Union. Whatever your interest, I hope all of you will come away from this speech with a richer understanding of the University of Florida.

I hope I've also conveyed how much Gainesville and Alachua County have meant to us over the years. We share a lot of trivia together, but our relationship is anything but trivial.

Building Bridges, Bridging Differences

Remarks delivered at a celebration of the University of Florida East Campus, November 29, 2011. (Ed Poppell introduced President Machen.)

Thank you, Ed. Today is a special day for you, isn't it? Some people here may not be aware, but this is Ed's second-to-last-day as UF's vice president of business affairs and economic development. Ed has been with UF for 40 years. His dedication and vision have been the driving forces behind the development of the East Campus. It really should be named the "Ed Poppell East Campus."

Welcome, everyone, to the East Campus of the University of Florida!

We're gathered here at a time when a divided federal government and lackluster economy have left Americans deeply pessimistic. It is clear to me that in this climate, our hometown of Gainesville stands out as an unusually thoughtful, focused, and united place to live. We have reason not for pessimism, but for a great deal of hope.

Moving in a direction opposite to our nation's capital, long-standing divisions in this community seem to be fading. Town and gown . . . east and west Gainesville . . . green versus conventional. These distinctions may have historical significance but they are less and less relevant today.

Yes, we have our disagreements. But what's truly remarkable in these fractured times is how little distance separates us—how we are building bridges and bridging differences.

This East Campus is part of this transformation.

For decades, this site was a quasi-industrial DOT research park and a polluted urban brownfield. It hasn't been very long since it changed hands. In fact, UF held the grand opening ceremony here on November 30, 2005—six years ago, tomorrow.

Since then, the university, with consistent support from the city, has utterly remade these one-dozen acres.

We cleaned up the pollution and refurbished and removed buildings. We built this 82,000-square-foot office space. Like all our new buildings, this one has earned a LEED Gold rating. It uses 43 percent less water and 22 percent less energy than required by code. I encourage everyone to check out the LEED plaque and the building after this ceremony.

A little later today, we'll break ground right over there for a 15,000-square-foot data center for UF's computer servers and network devices. We acquired the rights to an additional six acres, including three acres for a new, 160-spot parking lot on the wooded lot behind you. And, we're about to start work on a major new lab for our hurricane wind engineers.

The city has helped with everything from fiber optic cable to issuing permits. GRU's progressive Solar Feed-In-Tariff will make possible a 750-kilowatt solar system atop the office building.

When all the work is done, we will have invested at least $37 million at the East Campus—and we'll have 450 UF employees here.

This investment is good for UF, because our main campus is crowded with buildings and people, and the East Campus is convenient and quick to reach. But, we have another reason to be here. We also have a mission to help the community break down the economic and racial barriers dividing east and west Gainesville.

We believe that a prominent UF presence here will attract new businesses, new employers, customers, and residents.

Growth and new jobs will also accompany better services, such as easily accessed family medical care. To bring in more doctors and practitioners, we're at work on a new and expanded primary care center not far from here, at Northeast 16th Avenue and North Main Street.

The city and county are our partners in this redevelopment. And, I think now is a good time to point out, we are also collaborators on another inspiring project that is moving UF ever closer to the city's heart.

Slightly east of the main campus, the city, county, university, and community have united behind Innovation Square. There, we are working together toward a vision of bringing new life, new business, and new jobs between campus and downtown.

Together, in short, we are bringing together east and west, town and gown, sustainability and prosperity.

I commend each of you who have stepped up to provide such unifying leadership. I know and trust that you will persist. However polarized and intransigent are our national leaders, let's all continue to make Gainesville a model for reaching consensus—for building bridges and bridging differences.

In Praise of Alachua General Hospital

*Remarks delivered at a community tribute for Alachua
General Hospital on October 9, 2009. The hospital closed its
doors on November 1, after eighty-one years in operation.*

I am a relative newcomer to Gainesville, having arrived in 2004. But from my first few months here, I was keenly aware of Alachua General Hospital's standing in this community. AGH was Gainesville's first hospital. Its history is our history.

We already had a courthouse, post office, and library when AGH opened in 1928. The city grew rapidly, and AGH became its nursery. From the outset, AGH's doctors and nurses welcomed the babies who grew up to fill our schools, enter our university, and grow our workforce.

For decades, if you were in a car crash, needed a broken arm set, or an appendix removed, you came to AGH. That was as true for University of Florida students and faculty as others. Old newspapers are full of headlines about injured Gator football players getting patched up and recuperating at AGH.

But the hospital was much more than refuge for those seeking medical care. People attended dieting, health, and child-rearing classes there. The quote-unquote "Pink Ladies" of the Alachua General Hospital Auxiliary were well known. On Halloween, the hospital offered its X-ray machines to verify the safety of candy collected by our ghosts and princesses.

A community is stitched together with a thousand threads. Alachua General Hospital was a place they came together in a safe and sturdy seam.

In his remarks, Tim Goldfarb noted that the closing of AGH marks an end and a beginning.

I think you could put it another way: as it did with so many babies, AGH helped bring this city into being. And due in part to this hospital's nurturing, we've grown up bigger and stronger than anyone would have imagined 80 years ago.

Our population has swelled to 115,000 and our university has thrived, thanks in part to AGH's coddling. We have one of the best hospitals in the Southeast in the Shands at UF Medical Center—a hospital raised up on the history, knowledge, and expertise that developed at AGH.

We plan a technology incubator at the AGH site. We believe it will grow the hospital's legacy by helping to midwife new cures and treatments from research labs to the patients who need them.

I will not pretend that there is no sadness in ending the era of this origin of so many Gainesville people, ideas, and hopes. But Alachua General Hospital will always be a part of who we are and what we become.

We are lucky to have it on our birth certificate.

UF and Florida's Children in Need

Remarks at the Marion County Children's Alliance Annual Children's Breakfast, November 6, 2008

The Marion County Children's Alliance has a great reputation in North Central Florida as a champion of organizations that work on behalf of children.

Our sheriff, Sadie Darnell, has said, and I quote, "the Marion County Children's Alliance is very solid with strong leadership." She should know. She chairs our own budding children's alliance, which is being modeled on your group.

Not long ago, pediatricians at Shands Hospital treated a sick infant, and they requested a follow-up visit for the next day. However, the mother, who was from Ocala, could not make the trip back to Gainesville. She only had $6.

Such incidents have become common at our hospital, where specialty clinics serve kids from two hours away or more. The recent spike in gas prices was the tipping point, but the underlying hardships are rising unemployment, increased poverty, and more strained social services.

Unfortunately, I think things will get worse.

The financial markets remain jittery and states and cities are struggling. It's particularly bad in Florida, epicenter of the housing bust. I know people are hurting here in Marion County.

I know that E-One, Fluid Routing Solutions, and Merillat have closed plants, laid off workers, or plan to. Unemployment here has nearly doubled in the past year, reaching 8.5 percent in August. Ocala was recently declared to be in a recession, joining most of Florida and the rest of the U.S.

Many of you see the impact. More families who need cash to keep the lights on or put food in the fridge. More families losing their homes. More moms and dads who need intervention to keep a stressed situation from becoming an abusive one.

I was surprised to learn that your wonderful Food for Kids Back-pack program sends almost 600 schoolchildren home every Friday with meals to tide them over the weekend. Six hundred kids who don't have enough to eat at home! And this is only at the start of what will be a long recession.

At this point, you may be thinking, "what do Marion County's kids and the Children's Alliance have to do with the University of Florida?"

My answer is this. Although it is not always obvious, you and UF are connected.

Organizations in the Marion County Children's Alliance focus on issues ranging from youth mentoring, to substance abuse counsel-ing, to dropout prevention, to legal services, to recreation. The Uni-versity of Florida, while obviously not a child advocacy group, has similar breadth.

Like you, we touch children's lives in diverse ways.

Often, your work and our work intertwine.

Let me start with our most seemingly far-removed mission: research.

The University of Florida is a big national research institution. Last year, our 5,200 faculty members received $561 million in re-search grants.

UF experts tackle many topics close to your work: improving education in high-poverty schools, helping disadvantaged students achieve, and combating diseases that disproportionately strike poor kids.

I just mentioned your Food for Kids Backpack program. Childhood nutrition has become a major issue in this era of rising, preventable type 2 diabetes and obesity in young people.

More than a third of kids today are overweight or obese, and minority and poor children are hardest hit. One cause: the cheapest food is usually the most unhealthy, a fact not likely to change as the economy worsens.

Medical researchers in UF's Health Science Center are active in this key area.

For example, UF and the University of Miami together operate the Juvenile Diabetes Research Foundation Gene Therapy Center for the Prevention of Diabetes.

Our scientists have made interesting discoveries. UF experts on taste recently learned that children who suffer from chronic ear infections might be at greater risk of obesity. That's because ear infections appear to damage an important taste nerve in the middle ear, leading to a preference for fatty foods.

Research is really important to the University of Florida, but many of our faculty and students also strive to improve the lives of kids now. It's just what we as faculty do.

We do a lot of service work with kids—all kids, but also struggling kids. UF agricultural extension service's Florida 4-H program, which celebrates its 100th anniversary next year, traces its roots to agriculture and home economics.

But today, by far the highest percentage of the over 200,000 Florida 4-Hers are urban kids. Twenty percent are black, paralleling the state's population.

Children in need from Pensacola to the Keys are also involved in UF programs devoted to after-school enrichment and academic tutoring.

More broadly, for over four decades our Health Science Center and Shands Hospital have been this region's epicenter for children's health services.

We are often the only option for children with complex medical problems who need care from pediatric subspecialists.

But what I want to emphasize today is our commitment to uninsured or Medicaid patients.

Last fiscal year, Shands Healthcare provided over $115 million in charity care. Of 1,479 children admitted from Marion County last year, 1,028 were uninsured or on Medicaid—70 percent!

UF also provides specialty care to 2,600 Marion County children with special needs through the Ped-I-Care network of local pediatricians.

Discouragingly, the Commonwealth Fund last spring ranked Florida 50th among states on 13 measures of childhood health care.

Obviously, securing adequate medical care for disadvantaged children—for all children—dwarfs the University of Florida's capabilities. But we do what we can . . . when we can.

My background is in pediatric dentistry, so I am most familiar with the huge gaps in preventative dental care and treatment for poor kids. Nationwide, nearly 30 percent of poor preschool children have untreated cavities.

In Marion County, two years ago, our senior dental students, supervised by Department of Health dentists, handled nearly 600 children visits. We did not have a student rotation in Marion County last year, but I am pleased to say that we expect to resume in January.

In February, UF plans to open an $8 million, state-of-the-art pediatric dental facility in Collier County which is targeted at poor children. This came about as a result of a unique collaboration between UF, a Naples philanthropy, Edison College, and Collier Health Services, Inc.

I know there are similar needs elsewhere, and I hope we can develop innovative collaborations in other counties.

We also have a third mission: education. When it comes to the children we are talking about today, education is what sews our three missions together.

The College of Education is really where we see this happening.

I am sure you are all aware of the classroom training requirements for the hundreds of teachers who earn degrees every year.

But you may not know of the college's varied efforts to improve teaching in high-poverty schools.

One new program allows teachers in these schools to earn a master's degree, based on instruction from visiting UF faculty as well as online classes. About 100 teachers statewide are enrolled, with the first class of 30 graduating this year.

Here's the important thing: the program is free, on the condition that teachers remain in their school for five years.

This seeks to get at the fact that half of all teachers quit in the first five years, with high-poverty schools facing the worst attrition.

Let me conclude with a couple of thoughts.

First, my goal in giving you concrete examples of UF's work with poor children is partly to inform—but also to get across a sense of the possibilities open to you and your organizations for interaction with UF.

Recessions pose a cruel irony: more families need social services at precisely the time when government gets cut. We have already seen this cycle take hold, and it will take all of us pulling together to provide the alternatives.

In addition to all the programs I have discussed, UF has a huge supply of active student volunteers. So, whether you seek the advice of a UF expert, wish to establish links with a UF program, or simply need some enthusiastic volunteers, try us. As I said earlier, we are in this together.

My second thought is that the conversation about poverty and children almost invariably dwells on the problems—broken families, dropouts, medical and educational deficits, and so on.

But while poverty may be a stigma, it is not a crime. Many children raised in families with few resources grow up to become productive citizens and great successes—often with help from organizations such as those here today.

I am proud to say that I believe we have over 1,100 such students at the University of Florida, including at least six from Marion County.

We call them Florida Opportunity Scholars.

Luisa Betancur, a May 2007 graduate of Belleview High School here in Marion County, is one of our scholars.

Luisa, whose family is from Colombia, moved to Ocala about ten years ago. Her dad is a Paso Fino trainer. A sophomore at UF, she maintains a 4.0 average.

Luisa said, and I quote, "There are thousands of students throughout the nation who are very skilled, competent, and intelligent. However, they are not getting the education they deserve because of financial reasons."

In other words, give kids the opportunity for growth and success, and they will make you proud.

With the economy worsening, with an increasing number of worthy kids in need of a hand up, that should serve as our inspiration—and our guidepost.

We Are Gainesville

Remarks delivered at the Gathering for Peace,
Understanding, and Hope on the anniversary of 9/11 at
Trinity United Methodist Church, September 9, 2012

This gathering began two years ago after an attack against the Muslim faith brought international infamy to Gainesville.

We were stung by that attack, and we were dismayed that it could in any way represent our community to the eyes of the world. We felt compelled to raise our voices for the true values of our gentle and accepting college town—those of respect for people of all faiths, for mutual understanding, and a desire for peace.

Thankfully, this community does not face a similar incident this year. However, we have every reason to continue the tradition of this gathering.

That is clear from the terrible violence against members of the Sikh temple near Milwaukee. It is even clear from the acrimony that fills this presidential election year . . . when name-calling so often replaces dialogue . . . and when healthy disagreement gives ground to unhealthy division.

What I think people too often forget is that extremism does not begin as extremism. It starts like a small point of light, and, when fueled by hate speech we may prefer to just ignore, grows into a dangerous roaring fire. So as we remember those who were killed on 9/11, we must ask ourselves, how can we stand up against religious hatred and violence? How can we renew the give-and-take of thoughtful conversation and revive our innate spirit of unity as Americans?

Our advocacy for good may start out with seemingly small actions—first, by just listening to, and appreciating, one another. As it turns out, this is something that I think Gainesvillians have become very, very good at.

As with any community, Gainesville has its issues . . . but when we are our best selves, there is a gentleness and spirit of acceptance about our town that truly rises above the ordinary.

We see this unusual harmony here at this evening's gathering. So many people, from so many different faiths, joined together to call for respect, mutual understanding, and peace.

We see it in the growing movement to protect the natural springs that are the singular environmental treasures of North Central Florida—a movement that has united rather than divided the local business and environmental communities. I was impressed to learn that Trinity United is a part of that stewardship, protecting the beautiful spring that exists on this property.

We experience this harmony in the gathering unity of town and gown, with the University of Florida and the City of Gainesville working side by side to create a new creative community that will finally join the UF campus with the downtown.

We see it in our residents' support for the arts, including public support for maintaining arts and music instruction for the children in our public schools.

We live this harmony in the many charities that are the mainstays of Gainesville public life, from the Friends of the Library Spring Book Sale to the UF Community Campaign ... and in joint university-city efforts to bring new jobs and development to East Gainesville.

Two years ago, we began this gathering as a needed response to hatred and intolerance reaching out from our community to the entire world.

This year—and hopefully in future years as well—it is we who are doing the listening and the speaking for our community. We are Gainesville. Let us take this opportunity to renew our embrace and celebration of the gentleness and spirit of acceptance of this city at its best.

As we mark the 11th anniversary of the tragedy of 9/11 ... and as we strive to overcome the violence and divisions of the present ... those are qualities that can help keep our campus, our community, and our country whole.

8

A First Lady Speaks

Me and My Ten-Pound Title

*Remarks at the Association of Academic Women
fall meeting, September 13, 2010*

With apologies to all the diaper-changing male professors out there, I know that women in academe face special hurdles, such as juggling child bearing with seeking tenure. I am glad to do my part for the Association for Academic Women as you seek to lend a hand.

You've introduced me as "First Lady," which is accurate. But I have wrestled with that term ever since my husband, Bernie, got his first job as a university president. That was at the University of Utah, where we were before we came to Florida.

First off, it is just plain weird to have a *Pride and Prejudice* title in this era of *Eat, Pray, Love*! But the bigger head-scratcher is, there is no job description. As a result, everyone seems to have their own idea of the role of the First Lady.

Since we are all university people, in the spirit of scholarly inquiry, let me read you what a few authorities have said.

First Ladies, asserts the *New York Times*, are "those dutiful, ever gracious boosters in the president's shadow, who assemble the official dinners, keep the presidential mansion running smoothly and represent the university at events."

Well!

Lady Bird Johnson may have come closer to the mark when she said, "The First Lady is, and always has been, an unpaid public servant elected by one person, her husband."

But my favorite expert is Jackie Kennedy Onassis. Jackie insisted, "The one thing I do not want to be called is First Lady. It sounds like a saddle horse."

Amen. But perhaps unkind to horses!

I think what all these descriptions share is a discomfort with the link between marriage and power, one that has never seemed more antiquated than it does today. *First Lady*. It just about groans with the burdens of Victorian women of privilege.

No knock on those burdens, but had I chosen to embrace them when I became a First Lady twelve years ago, I *would* have been groaning. Well, I didn't. It took me a while, but I figured out my own definition for this title.

I am lucky enough to do what I want. What matters more, I can be a force for change for the things I believe in. That is not a burden. *That* is a bounty.

Today, I want to share a little about my personal journey, and what I and my 10-pound title have tried to achieve together. Hopefully we can have some fun and you'll hear a thing or two worth carrying out of here. After all, some of *you* may have First Husbands someday. Scratch that, thanks to Todd Palin, they'll get to be *First Dudes*. Now how unfair is that?

I'll start with a little about myself.

I was born the second of three daughters in St. Louis in 1945. My dad owned gift shops and my mom worked at our church. We were Catholic and I went to Catholic schools. My grandmother had always dreamed of being a nurse, and she imparted those dreams to me. I graduated from St. Louis University College of Nursing at 22.

That was in June 1967. I married Bernie on July 1. It was about 180 degrees, and in our wedding pictures, everyone seems to be melting. Bernie went to dental school at St. Louis. We met in the library, and on our first date, we went to a freak show at a fair. Looking back, it was kind of a sneak preview of university life! We said our vows at our church, with the reception held at the same home where I had grown up.

For most of my marriage I worked as a nurse part-time while raising our three children: Lee, Michael, and Maggie. I spent 27 years in nursing, most of it in neonatal intensive care units, where I cared for premature and ailing babies.

I loved my work. The NICU is specialized and intense and the nurses become very close. This helps explain why it was so hard when we left Michigan in 1997 to go to Salt Lake City for Bernie's first job as a president at the University of Utah.

I had stopped nursing a few years before, but this First Lady job, this was *totally* different. I wasn't on a team. I was alone, with only the cold comfort of my whale-bone-corset of a title.

There was no one to ask for help, because you have no friends when you move. And making friends in this position is hard! As First Lady, you have to worry about false friends, or becoming too close to wives of university VPs who might have to move on. And I am a woman who really needs my female friends!

At parties, standing next to Bernie, people were so eager to get close to him that they practically pushed me away. That's a funny feeling. I thought, why am I here? What is the point? I am not having a good time!

I played the hostess at official dinners and appeared at Bernie's side at university functions. I suppose I looked fine. But, inside I was floundering. Time passed, and slowly, without thinking about it, I just started to do what I wanted to do.

And that's when things finally started to gel.

I'll tell you a little story. My dad used to take me on trips out West, and I have always loved Western culture, and when we were in Utah I got into cowboy poetry. Pretty soon, I was heading out by myself to the National Cowboy Poetry Gathering in Elko, Nevada. Bernie would show up alone at university events when I was gone, and people would ask, "Where's Chris?" He'd tell them, "Oh my God, she is out there with those cowboys in tight pants again."

That wasn't a bad thing! The First Lady title automatically sets you up as a Stepford Wife, so people are genuinely relieved to learn you're a real person. In fact, and here's what finally sunk in, *that's part of my role as First Lady*.

Bernie is an introvert, and he doesn't display a lot of emotion, and he often has to be firm and distant. I think sometimes people look at me and think to themselves, "He can't be all that bad, because she's kind of nice."

If I can do that for him, that's a good thing for his leadership, and by extension for the university.

We were in Salt Lake six years, and I feel like I spent the whole time practicing. When we arrived here in 2004, I was more comfortable. But now I faced figuring out, all over again, how I could help at UF.

There's the expectation of the First Lady as hostess, and then there's the expectation she will help raise money for the university. And absolutely, I am glad to do my share. But I am a person who does not like to ask for money. I would much rather make friends than make asks.

If you think about it, though, the point of fundraising is to support the university. There's more than one way to achieve that goal.

We had been at UF about three weeks when I started hearing about a committee working on sustainability. It piqued my curiosity—as a family we had always recycled, and I am environmentally minded, but I didn't know a lot about sustainability. I asked Bernie about it, and he said it was important, but he was too busy putting out fires.

I started attending the meetings, and it became obvious that despite years of hard work, these folks felt stymied. One night, Charles Kibert, at the Rinker School of Building Construction, sent an email highly critical of quote-unquote "the administration." So, I called Charles up and I asked him where the bottleneck was.

He said, "It's the middle," meaning middle management. It was like a light went off. I said, *"Charles, I think I can do something about that."*

I talked to Kim Tanzer, former chair of the UF Faculty Senate and member of the sustainability committee and now dean of architecture at the University of Virginia. Kim suggested Bernie give a speech urging administrators and staff to pursue sustainability no holds barred. I said, "You tell him what to say, and I will make sure he is there."

I was sitting in the audience with Les Thiele, a political science professor who had chaired the committee, and he looked at me and said, "Do you know how long I have been waiting for this moment?" I just got chills. The *passion* of these people was finally amounting to something.

It took off like a rocket. We created an Office of Sustainability in Tigert Hall and hired our first director of sustainability in 2006. From there, we increased building energy efficiency, reduced greenhouse gases, made available transportation alternatives, planted native plants—the list just goes on and on. Today, UF is one of the greenest public universities in the country. We are routinely recognized by national groups from the Audubon Society to the *Princeton Review*.

Certainly a third expectation of the First Lady is that she will nurture the town-gown relationship. I have participated in several local organizations over the years. But my favorite is one I and a local veterinarian, Dale Kaplenstein, invented nearly three years ago.

Dale and I started a clinic together at the St. Francis House to provide care to homeless and very poor people's pets. You would be *amazed* by how people open up to you when you are helping their animals. We have discovered that if we can help these pet owners care responsibly for their pets, it's a step toward their owners taking better care of themselves.

I helped start this clinic because I am an animal person and because I thought it was an incredible idea. It didn't even occur to me until later that it fits under First Lady-slash-community-service. But you know what? That's exactly how it should be.

After twelve years, if I had to distill what I have learned into a single sentence, it is this: *people will always have expectations, but how you meet them is up to you.*

On that note, let me bring this to a close by confounding my own expectations, and perhaps yours as well. I am a passionate liberal, but I am much discouraged by the divisiveness and rancor in our current political life. So, I want to end with quote from a First Lady from the other side. I have to hand it to Laura Bush, because she said it best.

"The role of the First Lady," Mrs. Bush said, "is whatever the First Lady wants it to be."

Of Pets and People

Remarks to the Girl Scouts of Gateway Council,
May 18, 2012

I know that part of the Girl Scout Law is to be honest, so I need to start by confessing that I did not make my way past Brownies. I enjoyed my time as a Brownie immensely but only for about a year, when my family moved in second grade and my parents enrolled me in a Catholic school.

I got over the uniforms . . . and the rules . . . but my new school didn't offer Girl Scouts.

There are certain things you never forgive your parents for!

My time in Brownies was too brief, but I do remember learning that Juliette Gordon Lowe was a great friend to animals. I have always shared those feelings, and they have guided me to the most meaningful volunteer work of my life.

This is the work that I do here in Gainesville for St. Francis Pet Care, a free pet-care clinic that I operate with my friend Dale Kaplenstein—together with a group of the most warm-hearted, hardest-working volunteers in the world.

Every Tuesday, we provide poor and homeless residents with free, basic medical care for their pets, as well as access to spay and neuter services. We have treated more than 1,500 dogs, cats, and other animals, and we celebrate our fifth anniversary in September.

In that time, one of the biggest lessons we have learned is that our clinic isn't just for pets. Our clients have endured some pretty hard times, and their hearts are penned up tight. But by showing care and love for their pets, we are freeing those hearts.

We are reaching our clients with services they are too proud to ask for but desperately need—including medical care, legal advice, veteran's services, and assistance with domestic violence situations.

At a time when so many people are facing tough times, I am pleased that we can reach people in this way.

But our experience also says something about the nature of compassion. More than anything, our clients want to take care of their beloved animals. When they understand they can achieve that care by taking better care of themselves, they open up to the possibilities.

I believe Juliette Gordon Lowe would have understood this special magic—that animals can help us fulfill the Girl Scout Promise "to help people at all times."

I thank the Girl Scouts of Gateway Council and everyone here for sharing in that understanding, and I look forward to many more years of caring for the pets, and the people, of this community.

"Spokespersons for Freedom"

Remarks for Special Olympics ceremony,
St. Francis Catholic High School, December 2, 2012

We owe this occasion to Balance 180 Gymnastics and Sports Academy—a Gainesville nonprofit organization dedicated to helping children of all abilities participate in sports. There are a lot of imbalances in our community, our country, and our world. Thank you, Balance 180, for helping to make things right!

Some of you may know the Special Olympics traces its origins to the late Eunice Kennedy Shriver, one of the nine Kennedy children.

Mrs. Shriver grew up playing family sports with her sister, Rosemary Kennedy, who had an intellectual disability. That experience left Mrs. Shriver convinced that children with intellectual disabilities, like all children, gain a great deal of joy, self-esteem, and personal growth from sports.

Mrs. Shriver also recognized that she herself had learned a lot from playing sports with Rosemary. But in her time, there were distressingly few options for such children to participate in sports. So, Mrs. Shriver started a summer camp in her backyard. The success of "Camp Shriver" led to the first Special Olympics in 1968.

In the nearly half century since, Mrs. Shriver's backyard camp has become a global phenomenon—while always promoting the guiding principles that children with disabilities benefit from sports, and that children of all abilities learn from playing sports together.

Those are exactly the guiding principles of today's event—except that they are all the more relevant because of the young ages of these children.

Young childhood is a unique period, a period when we form impressions of ourselves and the world that last a lifetime. This is especially true of children in their most formative years, ages 2 to 7, the ages of the children we are celebrating today.

Every child this age deserves a chance to experience the exhilaration, freedom, and feeling of overcoming adversity that comes with sports.

Every child deserves the chance to bolster her or his self-esteem and intellectual development through sports.

And every child also deserves a chance to play with other children who look and act differently. There is no better preparation for the world they will encounter when they grow up—a world that is growing more diverse by the day.

Eunice Kennedy Shriver understood that while the Special Olympics is profoundly beneficial for children with intellectual disabilities, the concept benefits each and every one of us.

I would like to conclude with her words on that subject.

She said, and I quote, "Special Olympics athletes are spokespersons for freedom itself—they ask for the freedom to live, the freedom to belong, the freedom to contribute, the freedom to have a chance. And, of all the values that unite and inspire us to seek a better world, no value holds a higher place than the value of freedom."

In Celebration of the
Stetson Kennedy Collection

Remarks at a celebration commemorating the opening of the Stetson Kennedy papers in Special Collections, Smathers Library, October 22, 2013

I think perhaps we should begin by just appreciating this moment.

We live in a time of relentlessly virtual information. But today we're celebrating the physical writings, papers, scribblings, tapes, and photos of Stetson Kennedy. This collection is being made public in a library, an institution closer in spirit to ancient Alexandria than Silicon Valley.

No one would be more pleased than Stetson himself. For, among his many passions, he was an avid folklorist who collected and trumpeted the voices and stories of his own transformational times.

In his early twenties Stetson crisscrossed the Southeast for the Works Progress Administration, taking oral histories and documenting lives, a young Zora Neale Hurston at his side. The Stetson Kennedy Collection joins Hurston's papers, as well as those of their compatriot Marjorie Kinnan Rawlings, in Smathers Special Collections.

I served on the board of the Florida Folklife Council and am fascinated by our original cowboys, the Florida Crackers. As I share Stetson's interest in folk culture, I am proudly behind his politics. I deeply admire his trailblazing work on behalf of social justice and human rights and against racism, oppression, and environmental degradation.

Stetson Kennedy was so many things. A Florida boy who loved his state; a folklorist; a firebrand political activist; a journalist; and a lover of words and jibes who once said, "If something seemed to be wrong, I tried to cross swords with it, always on the assumption that the pen is mightier than the sword."

What's priceless about the documents Stetson and his pen left us is how vividly they reveal his many personas.

The collection dates to Stetson's high school days in Jacksonville in the early 1930s and stretches ninety linear feet to the end of his ninety-four years.

Its treasures include . . .

"Gin House Lake," a poem he wrote while at UF that appeared in the student literary magazine, *The Florida Review*. He has said he took a writing class with Marjorie Kinnan Rawlings. I like to imagine her pleasantly surprised by the poem.

His accounts of lynchings, Ku Klux Klan activities, and other harsh realities of Jim Crow life collected for the WPA's *Florida: A Guide to the Southernmost State*. Stetson believed he should write about the good and the bad for the guide, but these accounts were expunged from the final draft.

An astonishing collection of the various paraphernalia of the KKK—including all their secret signals, bylaws, and propaganda—

gathered as part of Stetson's decades-long crusade against the Klan.

In the 2000s, Stephen Dubner and Steven Leavitt, authors of *Freakonomics*, challenged some of Stetson's account of his famed infiltration of the Klan. But no one disputes that his courage and exposure of the Klan's secrets eroded its power, making it easier and less dangerous for the earliest Civil Rights workers.

Stetson's life was full of complications, mysteries and ironies. I discovered one of my own when a friend lent me a signed first edition of *Palmetto Country*, Stetson's first book. It contained this curious inscription:

> "Lost, strayed or stolen: 1 thorobred gal youngun; answers name of Ethyl. Finder please provide love and good home or return to Stetson Kennedy, 10/24/44 A. B."

I'll always wonder if the "Ethyl" in the inscription was a horse!

As I said, Stetson's life was full of complications, mysteries, and ironies. So I think it's fitting that his papers wound up in a library named in honor of a nemesis, Florida Senator George Smathers.

I understand that the Smathers and Kennedy families are good friends today. But more than a half century ago, Stetson opposed Senator Smathers for his support of big business and opposition to civil rights, and in 1950 he ran as a write-in candidate against Smathers.

This quixotic quest was memorialized in a song by his good friend, Woodie Guthrie.

One verse goes

> I ain't the world's best writer, ain't the world's best speller
> But when I believe in something I'm the loudest yeller
> If we fix it so you can't make no money on war
> Well, we'll all forget what we was killing folks for.

Senator Smathers may have his name on our library. But thanks to the preservation and public availability of these writings, papers, scribblings, tapes, and photos, Stetson will always be the "loudest yeller."

9

Of Nature and the Arts

A Historic Opportunity for
Our Most Precious Resource

Remarks at the UF Water Institute Symposium,
February 27, 2008

For most of our history, we have taken water for granted, at least here on the East Coast.

We have dumped prodigious amounts on our lawns and golf courses. We have allowed farmers and industry virtually unfettered access to our aquifers, lakes, and rivers. We have drilled, piped, or pumped to accommodate every new subdivision or housing development.

Water may be essential to life, but we are accustomed to abundance, and we continue to pay a pittance for it—unless it arrives in a clear plastic bottle.

This tradition is passing. With much of the country, including large swaths of the East Coast, in a historic drought, residents and policy makers are paying more attention to water than they have in years, if ever.

That is why your work here at the University of Florida Water Institute's first major conference is so timely and important.

As water scholars, environmentalists, utility managers, climatologists, and engineers, you make it your business to think about water every day. What has changed now, it seems to me, is that people are alive to the issues, and eager for your leadership. You have a historic opportunity to influence our laws, regulations, and customs with the best interests of our most precious resource at heart.

University of Florida faculty conceived the interdisciplinary Water Institute to bring to bear the university's myriad research strengths on discovering solutions to the complex and difficult issues surrounding water.

I hope this conference encourages that process, not just among the academics present, but with our many outside participants as well.

UF experts in the 1970s had a great deal to do with the creation of Florida's system of water management districts, today seen as a model for government stewardship of public water resources. I believe the time is ripe for this institution to join with public policy makers and private industry to make similar contributions again.

Rachel Carson wrote, "In an age when man has forgotten his origins and is blind even to his most essential needs for survival, water along with other resources has become the victim of his indifference."

With lake levels at or near historic lows from Lake Powell to Lake Lanier to Lake Okeechobee, with residents from West Palm Beach to Atlanta to Raleigh coping with water restrictions, and with crops across much of the country's southern plains stunted for lack of rain, I think we are shedding our indifference—for the moment anyway.

You couldn't be here at the Water Institute at a better time. I urge all of you to take advantage of this reawakening to lead us in protecting and conserving this life-giving resource for our children and grandchildren.

A Home in the Woods

Remarks written for the groundbreaking for the new
Austin Cary Forest Learning Center, April 6, 2013

It's been 17 months since the building that once stood here was destroyed by fire. People had gathered here for classes, retreats, conferences, and family events for a quarter century. They are still pouring out their sadness in correspondence with the university.

One woman wrote recently of her memories of her daughter's wedding in that simple cypress log building amid these woods. She ended her email with the words, "You have to rebuild."

I am pleased to be the first to say this morning, we will.

With the support of many generous donors and so many others who share a deep affection for this place, we begin construction today on a new learning center that will honor and expand the traditions of the old.

With a library, conference room, kitchen, and more, the new center will welcome more community school groups and youth organizations. More classes. More retreats and conferences for staff and faculty from across the university. And, I am sure, more weddings.

It will be an artful and useful building. But ultimately, people will benefit from returning here to Austin Cary Forest for reasons that go beyond shelter.

The 12-mile trip from Gainesville and the single-lane lime-rock road will lead, as before the fire, to the chance to reconnect with nature. The chance to enter the native Florida pine woods that are so close to us, yet in our busy lives, so seemingly out of reach.

Here, by Lake Mize, among these towering longleaf and slash pines, people feel calmed and refreshed. As though entering a cathedral, they get a sense that they are part of something bigger and more permanent, something beyond themselves.

I cannot think of a more ennobling lesson for all of us in this public university, dedicated as we are to education for everyone and the good of all.

As John Muir, the naturalist and author who championed preservation of so many of the greatest natural places in the West, once said, "Going to the woods is going home."

"A Very, Very, Very Fine House"

*Remarks at the "Roof Raising" for the George Steinbrenner
Band Building, August 21, 2007*

The University of Florida's first band was organized in 1913, seven years after the university opened its doors in Gainesville. There were 16 student musicians and a student director.

Performers played their own instruments, and practices were held in a spare classroom in Anderson Hall.

This didn't work out so well, because families who lived across University Avenue complained about the noise.

Making matters worse, President Albert Murphree's office was in Anderson Hall, a fact the musicians were not allowed to forget.

Today, the Pride of the Sunshine Fightin' Gator Marching Band counts 300 musicians in its ranks. And the marching band is just the largest of no less than 12 College of Fine Arts bands whose performers hail from all over this university.

Whether you are attending a football game or an evening performance, the renowned UF Wind Symphony, Symphonic Band, and other bands are at the heart of our athletic and cultural life.

But that drumming and brass melody you sometimes hear welling up from Norman Field . . . that's the sound of the marching band practicing the only place all the performers will fit—in the great outdoors.

It's been nearly 100 years, yet our bands don't have a home they can call their own.

Thankfully, this song has just about been sung.

The building whose construction we are celebrating today will finally give the bands their very own, very beautiful space to practice and perform.

The new George Steinbrenner Band Building will have a 5,600-square-foot rehearsal hall, room enough for every single member of the marching band and their instruments . . . and yes, that includes the tubas and sousaphones!

The acoustics will be state-of-the-art, enhancing the quality of the sound while leaving the neighbors unperturbed.

There will be 3,500 feet of storage space and a comprehensive, 1,600-square-foot music library. Lobby areas, offices, and a conference room will round out the interior.

What's more, this new building is part of a longer-range effort to renovate and enhance the entire School of Music.

Even as this university branches out into areas of education and research that our founders never dreamed of, the arts and music remain central to our mission.

In fact, this building is the second in a series of cultural art facilities that are being completed in concert with the university's strategic plan.

As is surely obvious from the name, the owner of the New York Yankees—a huge Gator fan—is the source of the generous donation that helped make this building possible.

Another big-hearted benefactor was Stephen Stills, a guitarist with Crosby, Stills & Nash, and a part-time Gainesville resident.

For his donation, we are naming the rehearsal hall the Stephen Stills Band Rehearsal Room. We are grateful to George Steinbrenner, Stephen Stills, and the many other donors who made this building possible.

Nearly a century ago, a handful of student performers practiced in a spare classroom.

Tomorrow, hundreds of musicians will fill a building that is on a par or superior to any band building at any university in this country.

If you love the sound of the marching band practices wafting across campus, rest assured, the band will still hold outdoor drill rehearsals. But as Crosby, Stills & Nash once put it, we will soon also have "a very, very, very fine house."

Art as Ambassador

Remarks at the dedication of the Harn Museum of Art
Asian Art Wing, March 30, 2012

Anyone who has picked up a paintbrush or a piece of clay knows it takes faith to make a piece of art. Perhaps what separates good artists from great ones is that great artists have an abundance of faith. They're passionate, and they believe in their work—even when no one else shares their passion or conviction.

Less than a quarter century ago, the place where we are standing tonight was an empty field far from the hum of life on our main campus.

It took faith to imagine a popular art museum here. And it took passion to build this museum into a center of arts and culture, a renowned university art museum, and a campus-wide student center—complete, as of tonight, with the Cofrin Asian Art Wing on the other side of the doors behind me.

We are all beneficiaries of the passion and faith of the Harn's generous benefactors, Mary Ann Cofrin and the late Dr. David Cofrin.

The Cofrins made possible the original Harn and its two expansions, and they also donated hundreds of stunning artworks in the Asian Art collection. Mary Ann Cofrin is here tonight with her five children and three grandchildren. Could everyone join me in recognizing Mary Ann and her family?

We are gathered this evening to dedicate the David A. Cofrin Asian Art Wing . . . and I know if I talk too long, you'll push me aside to get through those doors! I also know that David Cofrin is watching and he wants me to get on with it!

So let me make a simple observation: this new wing and the art it cradles is not ours to dedicate. Not really. Art is the expression of our humanity—our cultures and histories, our personalities and stories. Art belongs to everyone. It expresses who we are. Our role—really, our privilege—is to make that expression of humanity a part of the most enduring purpose of this university.

And that . . . ladies and gentlemen . . . that purpose is the education of our students.

How do we prepare our treasured students for success in the 21st century? This is currently the subject of urgent national debate about the character and content of higher education. We must equip students for this era of instantaneous global communication, economic upheaval, and rapidly changing cultural mores. On that we all agree. And, yet, there are vastly different opinions about how to shape university-level education to achieve that preparation.

At the University of Florida, we believe that art must be part of our toolkit. When students need to be prepared to live anywhere and communicate with anyone, art has a timeless legacy of initiating cultural contact—like the ceramic wares on display in the new wing, which remind us of the Silk Road where diverse peoples have crossed paths for 2,000 years.

Art broadens awareness. It can bring clarity and depth of field to one's career and personal life. And it can help to inspire a happy life, an outcome surely as important as economic success.

I want to tell you about a current UF junior named Kayla Shahum, who last semester visited the Harn as part of a class exercise.

The day of her visit, Kayla was thrilled to finally get away from sitting in a lecture hall. And she appreciated the chance to see and touch real art, rather than viewing it on yet another PowerPoint. . . . Has anyone else here seen one too many PowerPoints?

What mattered most for Kayla was the magical way the Harn opened the door to the uncomfortable topic of the class, which was grief.

Guided by Professor Jane Houston and Harn curators, the students looked at different artworks and talked about how they shed light on the many aspects of the grieving process. The discussion was honest and fresh . . . and it got Kayla thinking for the first time about the rich possibilities for art in her career.

You see, Kayla and her classmates need to become experts at helping others cope with grief. They aren't studying art, museum science, or art history. They are students of nursing.

To date this academic year, the Harn has welcomed Kayla and 3,566 other University of Florida students in class visits. The classes come from journalism, engineering, sociology, architecture, English, and medicine. They even come from IFAS. If you speak to these students or their professors, you learn that more than a few have experiences like Kayla's.

As Nigel Smith, a professor of geography who routinely brings his classes to the Harn, commented, "You can see little lights going on."

Those little lights may not be as measurable as standardized test scores. But they satisfy our deepest responsibility as educators, which is to open students' eyes to new and unfamiliar landscapes.

And today, no new and unfamiliar landscape may be more important than the one our students will confront in the growing countries of Asia.

We already have a variety of classes that revolve around Asia, study-abroad programs in Asia, and the UF Beijing Center. But that is not enough.

Works of art—the works of the weaver, the ceramics maker, the film maker—are ambassadors for their countries and cultures. If we want our students to know China, Korea, or India, we must introduce them to the countries' ambassadors.

The Harn's Asian art collection is rich and extensive, but most of it has been locked away in storage. With the opening of the Asian Art

Wing, we set these works free to continue their diplomatic mission to our students and the world.

Nothing I can say can match the experience of the five exhibitions in the new wing. So, let me simply note, there are about 400 works of art on display this evening, each carefully selected from the more than 2,000 pieces in the Harn's Korean, Chinese, Japanese, Indian, South and Southeast Asian collections.

The exhibitions tell many stories . . . of the jades of the Ming dynasty, of Chinese women artists of the 18th and 19th centuries, of the Silk Road.

What you won't see, but what you should know, is that the Harn is uniquely equipped to tell these stories. Its two dedicated endowments for Asian art acquisitions and its endowed curatorial position in Asian art make the Harn a leading university teaching museum for Asian art.

For our students and for us, the Asian Art Wing will be many things—a place to learn, to interact, to engage in quiet contemplation. But the art here also represents our passport to the landscapes and cultures that are most important to our future. As Professor Smith said, art turns on little lights.

Who knows what future awaits our graduates as they find their homes around the globe? The world is full of clashes of misunderstanding and conflicts of civilizations. But a shared understanding of art gives us a shared understanding of humanity.

Art promotes acceptance and appreciation. It gives us direction. It shows us an Earth the way it appears from space at night, with those little lights twinkling throughout every civilization.

Our Trees Ground Us

Remarks at Arbor Day Tree Planting Ceremony,
April 24, 2012

Good morning, and welcome everyone. It sure is a nice change to see a crowd outside Tigert Hall with no one holding up protest signs!

In just a moment, we'll plant that live oak, which was donated by Progress Energy. But, let me first note that before a university stood here, there stood trees. Old photographs, taken when we had just a handful of buildings, suggest that most were native longleaf pines. While the university's growth spelled the end of that forest, it began another.

Today, we have 183 species of trees on campus—an arboreal splendor that defines the University of Florida as distinctly as our buildings' Collegiate Gothic architecture.

Bluff oak ... Florida red maple ... flowering dogwood ... our trees include both natives and exotics, and many of them were planted by hand.

Few reveal the circumstances of those plantings, but we have some trees with pedigrees: the five live oaks honoring the victims of the 1990 student murders. The sycamore that people call the "moon tree" because it was grown from a seedling carried to the moon and back aboard Apollo 14. The "Tom Petty Tree"—a lime tree near Phelps Laboratory that is said to have been planted by Gainesville's native rocker when he worked on the UF grounds crew.

We also still have a few of those granddaddy longleaf pines, including one estimated to be 227 years old when it was designated as the "University of Florida Bicentennial Tree" in 1976.

Our experience shows that while we humans can destroy our natural woodlands, we can also help to preserve, restore, and create them. Indeed, that is exactly the purpose of Arbor Day, begun in Nebraska in 1872 to encourage settlers of the West to plant trees as windbreaks for fields, shade for homes, and orchards for fruit.

Here on campus, we have all relished the shade of our trees during this spring's drought. We love to stroll under them, we rush to snag the shadiest picnic tables at lunch, and we note with silent approval when their flowers or colors mark the passing of the seasons. Our trees ground us. They root our university in this place in the world.

J. Sterling Morton, the founder of Arbor Day, said, quote, "Other holidays repose upon the past—Arbor Day proposes for the future." Those words, of course, precisely match our own purpose at this university. What better place to realize them than here by Tigert Hall? At what better moment than this beautiful spring morning?

I thank Progress Energy for being a valuable partner to UF, contributing $3.5 million to numerous university programs, including the endowment that created the UF Water Institute. Progress Energy has also been a part of our sustainability efforts, and I thank them for bringing us together for this Arbor Day tree planting.

Planting Green Shoots

Annual State of Sustainability Address,
Smathers Library, April 5, 2013

If you are like my wife, Chris, and me, the arrival of spring makes you want to put down your electronic devices and head outside. Chris putters away in our butterfly garden, and I have some overly enthusiastic bamboo I try to keep a handle on. We're strictly amateurs in the garden, but neither of us can imagine a more pleasant way to spend a Saturday morning.

This time of year, people feel a need to connect with nature and its annual rejuvenation. I believe this springtime impulse reflects our basic human desire to live in balance with the natural world.

The sustainability movement's great strength is helping people to rediscover that balance. And just as spring gardening brings food and beauty to our homes and yards, so sustainability renews our planet.

Normally, we use Campus Earth Day to take stock of the university's progress on the continuing sustainability initiative. We'll get to that today. But with thoughts of spring gardening in my mind, and in consideration of your theme of "Green It Yourself," I want to first highlight a few students and faculty who are planting their own green shoots of sustainability at UF.

I'll start with a student named Stuart Block.

Stuart, a senior, wanted to do something about carbon dioxide pollution from power plants and its impact on climate change. After finding out how much electricity his own fraternity consumes, he spearheaded construction of a 10-kilowatt-hour array of solar panels on the roof. Beta Theta Pi's solar array is only the second to be built on a fraternity in this country.

A faculty member who has planted a seed of sustainability is Victoria Pagan, chair of the classics department.

She had the idea that she could get future professors to teach sustainability by reaching out to today's graduate students. So, she started a workshop for grad students about how to embed sustainability in their curriculums. The Prairie Project workshop has been popular with students from many different disciplines, and it will be held for a third year this spring.

A group of residents and graduate students at UF's Tanglewood Village nurtured their own sustainability shoots—literally.

The group created a garden that quickly became a hit with Tanglewood residents and their families. They've grown, and eaten, lettuce, radishes, scallions, and more. The residents plan to expand the garden this spring.

These individuals—and so many others like them—have collectively led this campus to the goals we set eight years ago, when the university formally committed to becoming a more sustainable institution. Under the leadership of the Office of Sustainability, UF has come a long way since that time.

We've built 40 environmentally friendly LEED-certified buildings, including 18 with a "Gold" rating. We've embraced local food in our dining halls, with a quarter of all of today's food from sustainable sources. We've greatly expanded the bus system. We've retrofitted numerous buildings for greater energy and lighting efficiency. And, with five arrays of solar cells and three more under construction, we're even generating some of our own electricity.

As the university continues these efforts, the experiences of Stuart Block, Victoria Pagan, and those Tanglewood Village residents suggest that a more profound transformation is under way.

As we approach the second decade of sustainability at UF . . . and as we welcome another beautiful North Florida spring . . . it's clear that the people of our campus community will seed and nurture the next era of green.

Consider that

. . .

Faculty and staff are sharing more and buying less. In 2012, the university saved more than $2.1 million that would have been spent on new purchases thanks to employees choosing to reuse computers, furniture, and office equipment.

We're throwing away less trash. Overall, waste disposal on campus has fallen 18 percent from 2005. That's all waste—down 18 percent. Of the trash people do create, more and more never reaches the landfill. Together, we recycled nearly 14,300 tons of waste in 2012, more than 38 percent of all we created.

More and more students are choosing to transform their passion for sustainability into their life's purpose. We graduated UF's first five sustainability studies students last year, and we have 26 students pursuing that major now. Nearly 80 students are minoring in sustainability studies.

Faculty created at least nine courses centered on sustainability, and they're also reaching out statewide. Extension faculty now teach a UF-created "Sustainable Floridians" educational program in four Florida counties.

More of us are choosing to eat locally. UF began its Community Supported Agriculture program in 2010, and about 200 people are now enjoying a spring bounty of cabbage, carrots, and lettuce from four local farms. Students and faculty have rented out nearly all the plots in our two campus gardens. Soon, we'll be picking our satsumas, navels, and valencias from trees growing around campus.

We're also embracing alternatives to the automobile. When classes are in session, campus passengers log well over one million trips each month on buses. There are more than 1,800 active members of the car-sharing service Zipcar—and more than 1,300 users of Zimride, a ride-sharing service. Biking on campus remains so popular that the university is installing new racks at dozens of locations.

I have more to add, but I don't want to keep anyone from their spring planting schedule! But before I wrap up, I want to take a moment to recognize one of the campus leaders in our sustainability efforts. Anna Prizzia, will you raise your hand so that we can all see where you are?

Anna directed the Office of Sustainability for more than three years, raising the profile of sustainability on campus, pointing the people of our diverse community in a common direction, and helping the university win numerous national awards for its sustainability efforts.

Anna also created the Florida Food Summit, aimed at getting more locally produced foods into schools and institutions. She left us last October to pursue that work full time at UF's Institute of Food and Agricultural Sciences. While we're getting close to filling her shoes with a new director of the Office of Sustainability, we'll never replace her. Will you all join me in applauding Anna?

To Anna, and to each and every one of you, thank you for all you've done to help us . . . share . . . conserve . . . recycle . . . educate . . . hop on the bus . . . and more!

The greater numbers we can bring together, the greater the impact we'll have on today's most urgent environmental problems—climate change, conservation, the growing scarcity of freshwater, and so on. In a season when we're busily planting and beautifying our gardens and yards in this *campus* community, I thank you for driving that greater and more lasting change in our *global* community.

10

In Tribute

A Tribute to "Miss Betty"

Remarks accompanying the presentation of the President's
Medallion to Betty Jones at Emerson Alumni Hall,
November 6, 2012

While I am pleased to have the chance to recognize all of you, my primary purpose today is to honor just one of you.

You might wonder, "Why only one?"

In almost any other situation, I might have to hedge my answer. But today, I can say with complete confidence that this employee is truly in a class by herself. We have 13,816 staff and faculty members at UF, but only one of those 13,816 . . . just one . . . has been employed by UF not 30 years . . . not 40 years . . . not 50 years . . . but more than 60 years.

We believe she is the longest-serving employee ever in the history of the University of Florida . . . and she's sitting right over there. Would you join me in applauding Betty Jones?

"Miss Betty," as some of you know her, arrived for her first day of work at the UF College of Education in September 1952.

That was before cell phones, before computers, before calculators. At that time, in fact, students still traveled back and forth to Gainesville via train to the old station downtown.

Television was new on the scene, and WUFT was only on the radio. Students couldn't buy beer . . . they probably drank it, but they couldn't buy it . . . because Alachua County was a dry county.

UF had become coeducational in 1947, but Betty worked here for six years before female students were finally allowed to wear shorts!

Today, Century Tower seems like it's been there forever. Betty remembers when it was built! She has seen the university quintuple enrollment from 10,000 to 50,000 students. She outlasted 10 interim and regular university presidents . . . and yes, it is highly likely I will be the 11th.

Betty spent her first two decades in the College of Education, then moved to the Office of Instructional Resources, which later became part of Academic Technology. She has been with Academic Technology for the remainder of her time . . . today, you will find her behind the reception desk at the office on the ground floor of Turlington.

And there, if you spend a little time with her, you will quickly discover the secret to her stability.

Betty makes friends with every student who approaches her desk. She loves faculty members and their families. She takes great pleasure in all the happenings of the university, large and small. In short, even after 60-plus years on the job, Betty remains full of love and appreciation for the life, people, and times of the Gator community.

Betty, I am told that when you were a young girl growing up in Live Oak, you wanted to be a teacher.

You achieved your goal . . . you teach all of us with your kind spirit, optimism, and continual sense of gratefulness for this wonderful place. And while 60 years is plenty, we won't mind if we're your students for many more years!

Our Brilliant Maverick

Eulogy delivered at the memorial service
for Dr. Robert Cade at University Auditorium,
December 5, 2007

I know a lot of people have been swapping stories about Dr. Robert Cade since he left us last Tuesday. I have a few to tell as well.

I want to begin with one of Dr. Cade's own stories, told in an oral history he gave to the late UF historian Sam Proctor.

Longtime Gainesville residents may remember that, about four decades ago, public school teachers walked off the job. Dr. Cade supported the teachers, but he disagreed with the strike, because he felt the teachers should uphold their contract.

So rather than report to Shands for his work as Gainesville's leading kidney specialist, Dr. Cade went over to Terwilliger Elementary School. There, he spent his morning teaching elementary students. When the kids went home for the day at 2 P.M., Dr. Cade put down his chalk and eraser and went back to the hospital to make his rounds.

This was the man the world knows as the inventor of Gatorade. He steadfastly pursued his own road, confounding all doubters. More than once, colleagues called his ideas "quirky."

But with Dr. Cade, that word translated as brilliant.

Dr. Cade's contributions cannot be overstated. In his leadership of the team of four researchers, who in 1965 invented Gatorade, he created the sports drink industry, while also coming up with a therapeutic beverage. Gatorade has earned the University of Florida more than $150 million in royalties. It also put this university on the map as a national research institution.

But this was not the work of a coldly methodical scientist bent over his laboratory equipment. Dr. Cade was a Renaissance Man, a physician, a crack scientist, and a creative thinker who followed his own path.

All were apparent early on.

He loved history and knew so much of it by high school, boredom in class led him to try to pass by just one point.

He ran the marathon, the real one in Greece, from Marathon to Athens while he was touring the world aboard a Navy destroyer.

Dr. Cade was an avid sports fan who chose St. Louis for his medical internship for one reason—so he could see the Cardinals play.

He played the violin from childhood.

He once ran for the Alachua County school board on a platform of integration.

With his son Stephen, he restored an old Volkswagen bug, using a Chilton's repair manual.

When it ran, he said, and I quote, "It was a bigger thrill than when we did our first kidney transplant."

When Dr. Cade was on a postgraduate fellowship at Cornell Medical School in Manhattan, he and his wife, Mary, drove a 1957 Studebaker. He said he liked that car because it belched out clouds of oil smoke, frustrating New York's tailgaters. You can see that car, one of 61 in Dr. Cade's collection, outside University Auditorium today.

So Dr. Cade was a sports fan, a devout Lutheran, a musician, an amateur mechanic, and—did I mention?—a poetry buff who turned a few verses of his own.

But here's what really counts: he had a tinkerer's curiosity and child's sense of wonder.

Early in his career as chief of renal medicine at UF's medical college, workers were moving rats into the animal quarters above his lab when they accidentally broke a crate. The rats took off everywhere.

So Dr. Cade promptly invented a live trap with doors that opened in, but not out. That trap caught all the escapees.

He invented a high protein popsicle, the Ten Plus Bar, to provide nutrition with the sweets. That popsicle evolved into something called Gator Go!, a high-protein milk drink.

Dr. Cade came up with a low-alcohol beer, Hop N' Gator, which was supposed to prevent hangovers. He crafted a hydraulic football helmet that protected players from concussions.

A few of Dr. Cade's inventions seem on the whimsical side. That is not beside the point. It is the point!

He never strived to be important. He simply followed his curiosity into whatever nooks or crannies it led him.

So when a volunteer football coach named Dwayne Douglass asked why Gator football players didn't pee during games, Dr. Cade was not going to brush off the question. With Jim Free, Dana Shires, and Alex DeQuesada, he set about teasing out the mystery.

It's a rich story after that, but the short version is that Dr. Cade and his colleagues came up with a drink to keep athletes healthy and energized.

The Gators started using their concoction in all their games, and by 1966 it had made headlines around the world.

The University of Georgia quickly came out with "Bulldog Punch." Florida State, if you can believe it, weighed in with "Seminole-ade."

But there was really no stopping what Jim Free named "Gatorade." More than four decades later, the sports and energy drink industry is worth $19 billion and dominated by Gatorade.

Before I close, I want to say a word about Dr. Cade and the university.

Our relationship was strained in the early years. But what matters today is not that conflict, but the fact that we resolved it, to both of our benefits. From our experience with Gatorade, we learned a lot about the right ways to support our faculty in nurturing their inventions.

Dr. Cade, for his part, maintained an active research career here until near the end of his life. It is thanks to his generosity that we were able to create an endowed chair, the Cade Professor of Physiology. We are deeply thankful for all Dr. Cade has done for the University of Florida.

At the request of the Cade family, I want to close with some brief words penned for this memorial by Neil Amdur, a former sports editor of the *New York Times*. It was Amdur who, as a reporter for the *Miami Herald*, wrote the first international news story about Gatorade 41 years ago.

Writes Mr. Amdur:

. . .

As a writer, I have spent a lifetime stringing words together into stories and sometimes editing the thoughts of others. But the words don't fall into perfect order when trying to define a man like Dr. Robert Cade.

The simplest explanation might be that he was a Renaissance Man, a quiet visionary who managed to push all the right buttons in pursuit of happiness. How else to explain someone who could be so generous on so many different levels?

Ray Graves, the former head football coach at the University of Florida, told me the other day that Dr. Cade "was doing what God intended for him to do, but didn't brag about it." Equally as important, I would say, is that Dr. Cade was "true to himself," which is really the measure of a person.

He served on so many levels—as a father, doctor, inventor, caregiver—that the joy he got out of collecting Studebaker cars seems almost like a small gift to himself.

What always struck me about Robert Cade was his self-effacing nature. So soft-spoken that I could barely hear him on the telephone. So sincere that you could feel his integrity. Yet woe to those who crossed him, especially when he knew he was right or felt he was being taken advantage of because of his beliefs.

I have always felt the true measure of a person's greatness—whether on a football field, in a classroom, or in the operating room—is whether they have enriched the world by their presence. Are we better off because of their contributions? Did they leave their business or profession, or, in a cosmic sense, the world, better than it was before they served?

Dr. Robert Cade is one of my heroes. He enriched us with his gifts. He gave us his intelligence and grace. But just as important, he gave us his humanity, his heart, AND his soul.

His legacy will live beyond this day. Among family, friends, and his dearly beloved university. And the countless millions whose lives he has touched in ways they may not even realize now. For that, we should be forever grateful.

Under Ed, the *Alligator* Roared

Remarks in honor of Ed Barber, longtime general manager
of the Independent Florida Alligator, *June 27, 2007*

The first edition of the *Florida Alligator* appeared nearly 95 years ago, on October 22, 1912. The paper read like a newsletter, with headlines about student clubs and other items of general interest. Its offices were next door to those of student government, and the relationship between the two was just as close. Published by UF, the *Alligator* debuted as a vehicle for university communication—also known as propaganda.

Ah, the good old days!

We are here tonight to celebrate Ed Barber, who retired this year from his position as general manager of the *Independent Florida Alligator* after more than 30 years.

We are honoring Ed with a Distinguished Alumnus award, though he never completed his journalism degree. He was too busy doing something more important: making sure this university and its student journalists had a real newspaper to read and write for.

In the late 1960s and early '70s, when the *Alligator* and the university were butting heads over control of the paper, Ed helped it emerge not only independent, but also on sound financial footing.

As general manager, he stayed out of newsroom affairs but was very active in business affairs. His sound and steady management allowed the paper to become what it is today: questioning, tough, fair, irreverent—and always willing to let young reporters and editors pursue their visions, despite the risks.

In other words, Ed gave the *Alligator* what it needed to be the kind of paper that can take a chunk out of my flesh on any given morning before I've had my breakfast.

Ed is one of those people who was born as what we used to call a newspaperman. A Miami native, he started his first paper when he was nine. In high school, he worked on the staff of the *Hialeah High Record*.

After a stint in the U.S. Coast Guard reserves, he started a career at a Miami bank, but it didn't agree with him.

With his new wife, Judy, and the couple's first child, the family moved to Gainesville. Ed enrolled at UF in the summer of 1963, living with his family in converted World War II barracks known as Flavett III.

It was an auspicious era for journalism. Ed took classes from two of UF's most famous journalism professors, Hugh Cunningham and Buddy Davis. In 1963, then student and editor David Lawrence wrote a series of articles criticizing the Board of Student Publications, which oversaw the *Alligator*. He was promptly fired. But the *Alligator* had stirred, and there was no putting it back to sleep!

Ed covered the Tigert Hall beat, earning a Hearst Writing Award for editorial writing in 1965. But with his young family, he needed to earn a living, so he started working in production. There he helped typeset stories, make half-tones of photographs, and do the other tasks needed to put out a paper in those pre-computer days.

When a spot came open for assistant production manager, Ed took it, dropping out of journalism school to do so.

His boss was Don Addis, the famous politician-skewering cartoonist, and one of dozens of well-known journalists who got their start at the *Alligator*. Another was David Lawrence, who I mentioned earlier. He became publisher of the *Miami Herald*.

But back to our story. By the mid-1960s, the *Alligator* was yanking at its tether.

In 1966, the Board of Student Publications fired three editors for, and I quote, "constant unprofessional harassment of Student Government officials and friends of the University of Florida."

In 1968, four editors quit after a dispute involving tenure for an outspoken liberal professor. The civil rights struggle, the Vietnam War, and student protests against the administration of President Stephen C. O'Connell only made times more volatile.

The *Alligator* and university were ripe for an abrupt and bitter split. And that's how people often tell the story. In that version, evil UF administrators kicked the *Alligator* off campus, where it promptly continued its noble quest for truth and justice.

But the breakup was a lot more complex, as Ed would be the first to tell you. What he might not say is that he may be the reason the *Alligator* survived it.

Most people here today know the split started with the 1971 publication of a flier containing a list of abortion referral services. Then editor Ron Sachs, now head of Ron Sachs Communications in Tallahassee, is one of our speakers today, and I will let him tell that story.

But I want to say this: following publication of that fateful list, both the university and the *Alligator* struggled mightily to find a way to cut the paper free while also ensuring it wouldn't go broke.

The *Alligator* needed UF student fees to keep printing—fees UF didn't want to provide without also having some control. The result was a long and drawn-out divorce, with more than its share of committee meetings, lengthy reports, and scotched plans. The process took 16 months to play out, culminating in 1973 with UF selling the paper to a private, student-controlled company called Campus Communications.

That sale, which included a large loan from UF to keep the *Alligator* afloat during the transition, occurred as part of a plan suggested by none other than Ed Barber.

It was Ed's plan that set in motion the *Alligator*'s new era.

But a funny thing happened. Those heading the transition naturally asked Ed to serve as the general manager of the newly independent paper. He wouldn't do it. He believed it was unethical to accept a position at a private company whose creation he had recommended while serving as a public employee.

As Ed told retired Journalism dean Ralph Lowenstein in an oral history, his fear was that he would, and I quote, "in effect, be creating with state money a position for myself in a private industry. I would be stealing state money."

It almost seems a quaint concern by today's lapsed standards. And it couldn't have been an easy decision, as Ed and his wife had just bought their first home. But he is an ethical man. Thankfully for us, two years later the *Alligator* held a national search for general manager, and Ed felt enough time had elapsed to apply. Of course, he got the job.

Some may wonder what Ed did in the ensuing decades to make the *Alligator* a success. Part of the answer is what he didn't do.

He didn't use the *Alligator*'s newfound independence to drive a wedge between the paper and the university. Instead, he maintained a healthy relationship, at least on the business side.

Unlike a lot of publishers, Ed also never meddled in the newsroom. He always kept a firewall between the business and editorial sides. Many newsroom alumni will tell you, they never saw him and barely knew him.

In the news business, that's not an insult, it's a compliment.

Ed stayed away from the newsroom even as he helped the paper prosper through business decisions like buying the *High Springs Herald* in 1990.

Editorially, the UF/*Alligator* relationship under Ed's tenure was . . . how shall I put it? . . . complex. The paper has covered this university fairly, insightfully, and comprehensively. Also, on occasion, not at all.

As for our differences on a day-to-day basis, I will only say this: sometimes it's best to take a long view.

Whenever I read something that causes me concern, I try to remember that the net result of the *Alligator's* scrutiny has been to strengthen and improve this university—the way any good newspaper strengthens and improves its community. Even when presidents and their cabinet members get exercised about it.

The *Alligator's* reach has also extended beyond Gainesville. It's hard to understate the importance of the paper to UF student journalists who later made important contributions to public life.

The paper's long list of important alumni includes not only David Lawrence, Don Addis, and Ron Sachs, but also Carl Hiaasen, several Pulitzer Prize winners, and many, many other journalists at this country's finest newspapers and magazines.

A lot of these journalists have said working at the *Alligator* was critical to instilling their passion for the field and launching their careers. There is no reason to doubt them.

Ed had an amazing career at the *Independent Florida Alligator*. He wrote for the paper. He labored to produce each edition. When times got tough, he helped to save it. He kept the paper sound financially, enabling its editors and reporters to do their jobs. Through myriad controversies and setbacks, he stuck with the *Alligator* and its staff, covering the news and shaping the lives of hundreds of young journalists.

Under Ed, the *Alligator* roared.

If there's any feat worthy of a Distinguished Alumnus award, this is it.

Mr. Ed Barber, in recognition of your distinguished and honorable career in journalism, your dedication to the highest and most ethical journalistic standards, and your long-standing commitment to the *Independent Florida Alligator*, ensuring that student journalists at the University of Florida have a well-recognized and respected newspaper at which they can learn their craft, it is my honor to present you with the University of Florida Distinguished Alumnus Award.

11

Our Past, Our Future

Toward UF as a Global Beacon

Excerpt from the State of the University address,
August 26, 2010

As we look to the future, we need to move toward the idea of the University of Florida as a global beacon—an institution attractive and accessible to students and faculty around the world and in cyberspace.

Bear with me as I unravel my argument.

Like many of you, I spent part of the summer traveling, including a couple of weeks in Asia. I visited South Korea, and then China, where I stopped at the University of Florida's Beijing Center for International Studies. From Beijing I flew to East Central China. There, I visited Zhengzhou University, with which we are establishing research and education partnerships.

ZZU, as they call it, is the top university in Henan Province and one of about 100 being groomed to be China's leading research universities.

The Chinese leadership is *pouring* money into these universities. Countries elsewhere in Asia, the Middle East, and Europe are doing the same with their own research universities, all with an eye turned toward creating equals to our own.

The financial balance of power is shifting. We see state support for U.S. public universities declining while other countries are vastly increasing investment in higher education. At some point, the best universities in China or Saudi Arabia will be competitive with our own—*at their campuses and online.*

UF is an excellent university with a promising future. We had a terrific year last year. However, the world is not going back to the economy of the last two decades. Our current, somewhat advantaged financial situation is only temporary.

We cannot ignore the emerging global marketplace in higher education. Sooner or later, it will force us to change. We will need to move away from the notion of UF as a university based in Gainesville, Florida, the United States, the Western Hemisphere. We will need to move toward a UF that students can attend regardless of where they live—physically where possible, digitally everywhere. We will need to complete a transition we have already set in motion, from UF as a global presence to UF as a global beacon.

For most of the last century, we were the state's biggest and most powerful university. We owned higher education here. This has changed in the last 20 years, as the other universities in the state have set about trying to imitate UF.

We have responded aggressively, concentrating on research and graduate education, building one-of-a-kind facilities, and aggressively marketing our singular brand.

This strategy has worked. We have established preeminence on our terms. Choose whatever indicators you want, and our hallmarks are quality, depth, and diversity. Even during this downturn, we remain separate from other public institutions.

But, just as the growth of Florida's other universities forced UF to adapt in the past, we must now adapt to the growth of new competitors in higher education—competitors nationally, internationally, and in cyberspace.

In other words, the game is changing on us, again. And, though it won't happen immediately, if we don't adapt to these new circumstances, we risk falling behind. That's the risk. If we play our cards right, these changing circumstances could solidify UF as a leading higher education institution of the world. *A global beacon.*

For-profit universities that offer online degrees are growing exponentially. And, traditional universities around the country are also expanding online. This is happening even at the most highly regarded institutions, such as those in the University of California system, including Berkeley.

UF had 28,000 applicants for about 6,400 spots this fall, which might appear to provide a cushion against online competitors. But, the history of the Internet is filled with sad tales of industries that misjudged its transformative powers. We do not want to follow the path of the music industry, newspapers, or the bricks-and-mortar retail industry.

Even if you think there is something sacred about the UF campus—okay, let's stipulate there *is* something sacred about the UF campus—it should be obvious that we have an opportunity.

We are practically built out. A downward slide in state resources seems inevitable. We already turn away highly qualified students because we don't have room. The technology is improving, and we can only increase access by enrolling students online, or at other locations.

To facilitate this change, we are seeking a distance education infrastructure company to help us increase the 52 programs we now offer online.

The company we engage will take charge of the mechanics, with faculty and departments providing the course content and maintaining academic control. Our experience with distance learning so far is encouraging. *The Economist* magazine recently named our online executive MBA program one of the top two in the world.

At the Warrington College of Business, participating faculty have seen pay increases. Other colleges have used online revenues to add faculty and staff.

Online expansion of our programs will magnify these kinds of benefits. And, again, if we don't satisfy the online demand, other universities will.

The same considerations motivate a related consideration: physical expansion beyond the Gainesville campus.

There is demand at Santa Fe College, so we created two degree programs there, one in business and the second in sports management. We are likely to add more. We just completed a UF at Santa Fe center, the "Gator Den," to give our students a home away from home.

We are discussing similar UF centers at Edison State College in Fort Myers and Miami Dade College.

We have also created a master's degree program in architecture in Orlando. So, the possibilities are not confined to undergraduates. Nor, in fact, only to students.

Orlando is home to our first major research building away from Gainesville, to be built adjacent to Sanford-Burnham Medical Research Institute. With groundbreaking planned for later this fall, we will have a comprehensive drug development center and biomedical research labs. This will give us a position of prominence in a key emerging biomedical center.

UF faculty members have long pursued research with a global perspective and collaborators. What Burnham represents is an institutional priority to involve UF where important research activities are under way.

When we expand outside of Gainesville, we open up additional space on campus. In particular, we make room for more paying out-of-state and international students.

There is no shortage of demand. Our own international under-graduate and graduate numbers grew *83 percent* in the last decade, soaring from 2,209 to 4,056 students.

We are also sending more U.S. students abroad. In 1999–2000, 1,065 UF students went to other countries. A decade later, that number increased *100 percent* to 2,158. We want to continue these trajectories, which is part of the role of our centers in Beijing and Paris.

Generally speaking, Gainesville is a welcoming destination for our international students. This brings up a matter of current local importance I need to speak about.

Students come to UF from more than 100 different countries, including many that are Muslim. In fact, UF's fifth-largest group of international students hail from Turkey, a Muslim country.

You have read about Gainesville's Dove World Outreach Center's plan to burn Korans on September 11. I want to share my personal opinions about this action.

Imagine what impression it will make on our Muslim international students who are spending their first weeks in America. Put yourself in the shoes of their parents, thousands of miles away, watching on TV what has already become an international spectacle.

Purveyors of intolerance do all kinds of harm, including making people feel unwanted and demeaned. We can't let that happen, not to our international students, not to our domestic Muslim students, and not to anyone in our community.

Several student and community groups are planning peaceful responses. I applaud these groups for reminding the world that the University of Florida and Gainesville welcome and treasure people of all faiths, origins, and races.

Let me wrap up my presentation with a last thought about UF's global road ahead.

Our online and state college expansion are part of what I see as a fundamental shift in higher education. This shift will put reputation and accessibility above city, state, or country.

Author Ben Wildavsky writes about this trend in his new book, *The Great Brain Race*. Wildavsky suggests that future students won't care if the university is in Singapore, Germany, or the U.S.—or even if it exists at all. They will simply expect to attend the school that fits their pocketbooks and dreams. Much the same will be true for scholars and scientists: already, they are placing institution above country or continent.

We attract students with 4.0-plus GPAs. We hire faculty from the Ivy League. We are *already* the university of choice for great students and faculty. We can, and should, tap into even more of the best and the brightest—wherever they happen to live on the globe.

Distance learning, physical expansion, new home bases for research: whatever steps we contemplate, I hope you will join with me in elevating UF from a university with a global presence to one that serves as a global beacon.

Our Morrill Act Tradition

State of the University address, August 30, 2012

Someone once said that summer is, quote, "when laziness finds respectability." Well, in that context, I think Chris and I were a little too "respectable" the past two months. We hung out around Gainesville while Gators were breaking records all over Europe—and not just at the London Summer Olympics.

In July, physicists at the particle accelerator near Geneva announced the detection of the last piece in the puzzle of our universe, the Higgs Boson . . . a.k.a. "the God particle." That historic milestone was shared by more than three dozen UF physicists, who together comprised one of the largest teams on the project.

Then, in London, athletes with Gator ties won 21 medals at the Olympics. If UF were a country, we would have outperformed Canada and Spain!

The Gator Marching Band won superlatives, too, as the only U.S. college marching band that performed at the Summer Games.

We were the world leaders, and we also met some world leaders. What an honor for the band and for UF! Now, that's respectability.

As you are no doubt aware, I've announced this will be my last year as president of the University of Florida. But, we are not yet ready to dwell on that ending. So, I want to start my address today with new beginnings by introducing the outstanding women and men who are experiencing their first year as new leaders at UF.

Three of these leaders are not able to be present today. They are David Norton, vice president for research; Diane McFarlin, dean of the College of Journalism and Communications; and Nick Place, dean for extension and director, Florida Cooperative Extension Service.

As I call the names of those who are here today, would you please stand:

- Dave Kratzer, vice president for student affairs
- Curtis Reynolds, vice president for business affairs
- Kelli Brown, interim dean of the College of Health and Human Performance
- John Hayes, dean for IFAS research

Please join me in welcoming all our new leaders with a round of applause.

As you greet your students and colleagues, new and old, I hope you are experiencing the sense of excitement that accompanies this time of year. We have a great entering class, terrific new faculty members, and much to anticipate.

However, it is also understandable if you feel some concern about the future. We begin this year under the shadow of the grotesque events at Penn State, the administrative tumult at the University of Virginia, and increasing concern over the cost of higher education and high student debt. Here in Florida, political support for universities is wobbly, and state funding remains anemic.

You may also feel some uncertainty about the search for a new president. But, I want to assure you that my successor will inherit one of the best jobs in the nation.

The University of Florida is in a strong position amid these uneasy times—a stronger position, in many respects, than our peer public universities in other states. We also have a clear map for our future—a map first drawn 150 years ago this year, in an era that was far darker than our own.

When we wrestle over the present, it often helps to remember the past. So, let me ask you to journey back with me to the summer of 1862.

In that summer, the country was in the midst of a Civil War that was becoming bloodier by the day. And yet on July 2, 1862, President Abraham Lincoln and the Congress gathered to enact an extraordinary piece of legislation. The Congress passed, and Lincoln signed, the Morrill Act, the law that created the land-grant universities. Those universities would come to include the University of Florida.

The Morrill Act is named after its sponsor, Vermont senator Justin Morrill. It deeded federal land to the states to sell, so that they could raise the money to found their land-grant universities. And, the act established those universities' mission and purpose.

You received a card when you came in today. On one side of the card is a quote that summarizes that mission. Quote " . . . In order to promote the liberal and practical education of the industrial classes in the several pursuits and professions in life . . ."

That idea of both a liberal and practical education is also the foundation of the University of Florida. That is clear from the quote on the other side of your card, which comes from the speech given by Nathan Bryan at the 1906 opening ceremonies for UF here in Gainesville.

Bryan later became a U.S. senator from Florida, but at the time he was chairman of the Florida Educational Board of Control. Speaking about the purpose of public education, he said . . . quote . . . "The country is governed by the will of the people, and in order to have good government we must have intelligent wills, trained minds, educated intellects."

The Morrill Act had three pillars. First, land-grant universities would be accessible to ordinary Americans, not just elites. Second, they would provide a broad education, adding agriculture and engineering to classics and liberal arts. Third, the universities would be controlled by their states and promote state and national progress.

As we face the considerable challenges of the present, I think it is revealing to discuss where UF stands within the context of these three pillars of our land-grant tradition—(1) access to education, (2) a broad college education, and (3) the promotion of state and national progress.

My remarks today preface a celebration of the sesquicentennial that will continue across the UF campus throughout the year, culminating with a major symposium in the spring. You will hear more about this celebration later today.

I will start with the first of three Morrill Act pillars, access to college.

We in the academic community talk a lot about all kinds of challenges facing universities. But in the public square, one concern towers over others.

That concern is rising tuition and student debt. The heat became more intense this year. President Obama decried tuition increases in the State of the Union, and headlines announced that Americans' student debt exceeded $1 trillion.

As a large, very visible state university, the University of Florida is easily swept up in the national outcry about high cost. But, with tuition of $6,143 for this fall, we do not belong with those identified as high cost and unaffordable.

Last year, our tuition was 31 percent below the average for four-year public institutions. We have the 45th lowest tuition of state universities. While 37 million Americans are saddled with college debt, 61 percent of UF students graduate with zero debt.

You are no doubt aware that UF's affordability has serious shortcomings when it comes to operating the university. But at this moment in history . . . when frustration over college debt is so intense that some question the value of attending college at all . . . our low cost keeps us attractive to families and it mutes our critics.

Our affordability also vaults us to the top of the most prominent rankings for value, from *Kiplinger's* to the *Princeton Review* to *Money Magazine.*

We will most certainly continue to raise tuition. Indeed, while other universities have hit the ceiling, we have some headroom.

At the same time, we will remain committed to the Morrill Act pillar of access, which has enabled us to educate more than 370,000 people—most of whom are from the ordinary American families Senator Morrill and President Lincoln so wanted to serve. We should recognize that today, those people include women, minorities, and other segments of society that could not attend college in 1862.

Our commitment to access includes UF providing millions in financial aid, as well as generous scholarships such as the Florida Opportunity Scholarship, to those who cannot pay for college.

Let's move on to the second pillar of the Morrill Act, which is that education should be broadly defined.

I am so proud of the quality of students at UF. This fall's 6,335 students continue the trend, with an average GPA of 4.2 and SAT of 1891, both up from last year. More than one-third of these students graduated in the top 5-percent of their high-school class.

With such high academic accomplishments, these students have many options for their college education. They choose UF because of our excellent faculty, great residential student life, and UF's extraordinary diversity of educational possibilities spanning 97 bachelor's degree programs. From astronomy . . . to dance . . . to graphic design . . . to mathematics to one of our newest majors . . . sustainability studies.

Some of today's loudest higher-education critics accuse universities of offering too many programs. They are especially scornful of programs that do not present a clear path to a job, insisting that universities should funnel students into vocations.

We are proud that UF produces one-fifth of the state of Florida's undergraduate STEM degrees—and nearly half of its graduate STEM degrees—in fields where job opportunities are so plentiful.

We are also proud that, whatever their field, nearly 40 percent of UF seniors in the class of 2012 already had accepted a job offer before they graduated.

But we also have faith in the inherent value of degrees in liberal arts and the social sciences.

Steve Jobs shared this faith, as does John Hennessey, an engineer and the president of Stanford University. As President Hennessey said recently, the loss of the liberal arts would be, quote, "a loss to the country."

I think President Lincoln and Senator Morrill would agree.

The final pillar of the Morrill Act is that land-grant universities help their states and the nation flourish. At UF, we affirm this pillar through education—and also through research.

I am happy to announce today that contracts and grants to the University of Florida for the just-ended fiscal year totaled $644.3 million. That is up 4 percent from last year's $619 million and an all-time high for this university in terms of regular funding.

We owe credit to the faculty for achieving this increase even as the economy struggles and federal agency budgets remain flat.

Looking ahead, we continue to build our research capacity through new bricks-and-mortar additions—and soon, a virtual one.

By the end of this year, UF will upgrade its research network to 100 gigabytes, accelerating the speed of data transmission by a factor of ten. We join only five other universities nationwide to complete this upgrade this year.

In the same way that land-grant universities once brought agricultural research to isolated farmers, today we spin off new technologies and new companies to the workplace.

We opened our newest technology incubator, the Innovation Hub, in January. Already, the Hub is nurturing 24 infant university spinoff companies.

Here are a couple of photos that capture the evolution of our Morrill Act mission of research that promotes state and national progress. On the left, a picture of campus from around 1915, with a field of experimental plants not far from Newell Hall. On the right . . . taken in 2012 and just a few blocks away . . . a contemporary snapshot of the Innovation Hub.

We are also improving the graduate education programs that sustain our research and innovation.

Last year, I discussed a university-wide initiative to revitalize graduate programs.

In July, a committee issued a report identifying excellent programs and programs with significant deficiencies. It may be time to reward those graduate programs that are truly exceptional. And it may be time to eliminate some programs that have not, and are not, performing up to the standards expected for our university.

As we work to fulfill the goals of the Morrill Act, the strains on public higher education have rarely been higher. In particular, state support for universities is falling around the country, with the State of Florida reducing its allocation to UF by some $219 million over the past six years.

To remain on our current trajectory, we need to increase our efficiency. We must do more with less!

Operational reengineering is ongoing, with our College of Liberal

Arts and Sciences expecting to save nearly $800,000 annually with its pioneering shared services center. In the aggregate, UF has reduced its operating budget by $100 million.

Further, we are adapting to take advantage of new technology in delivering online higher education.

As I speak, UF is in discussions with Coursera, the California-based online education company that is a leading provider of "Massive Open Online Courses." We are seriously considering an agreement with Coursera, which already includes 16 prominent universities, including UVA, the University of Michigan, and Duke University.

The Coursera style of education is very new, and no one knows how it will evolve. Even as we become part of this experiment in higher education, our fee-based Internet education enterprise has expanded to more than 6,700 students.

We believe we can increase tuition revenues through high-quality Internet offerings to students around the globe—without taking away from the residential campus at the core of our undergraduate experience.

As I wrap up, I want to respond to those who believe that UF and other land-grants should scale back in response to these difficult times. They think we should cut our course offerings, rein in our research ambitions, and become more insulated in our worldview.

UF is grounded in the Morrill Act. Always has been. It is not our tradition or our mission to be a confined or utilitarian university. It is not who we are today. And it is not the path to a thriving future for this university, this state, or this country.

Our trajectory embraces the faculty and students who made history at the particle accelerator in Switzerland . . . and the agricultural scientists who have made such life-altering improvements to citrus, peanuts, and tomatoes . . . and, as Isaac crosses Louisiana, the civil engineering researchers who are designing homes to better withstand hurricane-force winds.

Amid the backdrop of the current challenges to higher education, UF's future depends on our ability to reach even further . . . to stand up for the rich breadth and scope of the research and teaching legacies foreseen by Justin Morrill and Abraham Lincoln . . . and to prove our value with excellence and purpose, as we have done for the past 150 years.

Inventing Our Future

State of the University Address, August 22, 2013

The beginning of the fall term always reminds me how glad I am to be at this university. When I see the excitement on students' and families' faces; when I hear the band warming up; when I feel the energy of thousands of young people streaming through Turlington Plaza . . . all these things remind me that college campuses truly are sanctuaries.

The poet Robert Frost used to spend his winters in Gainesville and hold poetry readings on campus. I'd like to think his experience here inspired one of his most memorable lines. "College," Frost said, "is a refuge from hasty judgment."

Yet this particular fall, we all understand the refuge of higher education is vulnerable to judgments, both hasty and harsh. The very notion of college is under attack from the left and the right, hit by change on every front. The rise of online learning. Growing financial pressures. Open skepticism of our value.

Whether we like it or not, we need to respond. Our very existence is being challenged. And, the best way to do so is to get out front; to actively create our future by drawing on the essence of our history.

We can't just hide from these difficult times or react to them. We need to use the principles of access . . . academic excellence . . . a broad liberal education . . . and research for the good of the world.

We must seek to invent our own future—drawing on the strengths and missions of our past.

Our future includes online education. At UF, we are creating a four-year online undergraduate program, the E-Campus.

This is part of our renewed focus on the art and science of teaching undergraduates, and we believe the E-Campus will grow our historic legacy of academic excellence—both for online students and for students here on campus.

We are also seeking to invent, for these complicated times, a broad liberal education for students. We're building a UF core curriculum to create a unique shared experience for freshmen. We want to get students to think deeply about themselves and their world. This contrasts the vocational approach so en vogue, but we feel it gets at the true value of college.

Finally, we're enhancing our position among public universities, reinventing our highest tradition as a research and graduate institution that contributes science and knowledge to better our world.

We embark on the E-Campus, on the signature undergraduate experience, and on our drive to reach the next level of research universities from a solid foundation. We are inventing the future based on the strength of the past as a public land-grant institution.

Our campus continues to grow with the opening this month of the Clinical and Translational Research Building. UF's research computing capabilities have been newly fortified with the Eastside Data Center, its supercomputer HiPerGator, and our 100-gigabit connection. Shands and UF have merged as UF Health. Our Sid Martin Biotech Incubator was named the 2013 Incubator of the Year in the world. We are within a few weeks of groundbreaking on the renovation of the signature Reitz Union.

We also have several new leaders to help shepherd UF through these uncertain times. As I call out your names, please stand:

- Julie Johnson, dean of the College of Pharmacy
- James Lloyd, dean of the College of Veterinary Medicine
- Anna McDaniel, dean of the College of Nursing
- Thomas Pearson, executive vice president for research and education at UF Health
- Boyd Robinson, interim dean of the College of Dentistry
- Matt Williams, director of sustainability

Not attending today is Michael Reid, dean of the College of Health and Human Performance.

Thank you! Now, I believe our lawmakers also deserve some recognition for their contribution to this year's strong start.

For the first time in five years, the legislature did not cut our budget. We actually received new base funding from the state.

Also for the first time, Governor Rick Scott and the legislature recognized UF as the state's highest-achieving university. They put their support behind UF advancing into the ranks of the top public universities. And, they made UF the state's provider of online higher education for undergraduates.

After so many tough years, this legislation will help rejuvenate some of the departments most harmed by five years of cuts. It represents a new beginning.

With that new beginning in mind, let us look closer at the E-Campus.

By recognizing online learning as a new reality, the legislature's vision is to improve access to college and reduce its cost. By law, all Florida online students will pay only 75 percent of regular tuition.

That's the state's side of things. On our end, we begin the E-Campus with some experience, having offered online degree programs for years. In fact, we already have 7,000 online students!

Most are graduate level, but we also have 10 online quote "two-plus-two" programs. These allow associate-degree holders to attend UF online as juniors and seniors to earn their bachelor's.

For the E-Campus debut in January, we will expand five of these programs to four years. After that, we anticipate adding five more programs annually.

We are one of the first bricks-and-mortar universities out of the gate to go after first-time, first-year students. To be successful we must master two challenges.

One is to meet the legislature's expectations by expanding our tradition of access. We need to attract students to the E-Campus! And the second challenge is to enhance our legacy of academic excellence for both the online and the traditional students.

Let me take these one at a time, starting with attracting students.

When you look at students and graduates of UF's two-plus-twos, it's clear online programs appeal to those who otherwise could not be Gators.

In microbiology and cell science, consider Christy Richardson, a Port St. Lucie mother of three who couldn't leave family and home to move to Gainesville. Or Andrew Stygar from Vero Beach, who is the first in his family to attend college and didn't want to leave his job.

Or a young woman who earned her AA degree while still in high school and is now pursuing her UF degree while living at home with her parents.

This is 20-year-old Tanya Gorniewicz.

Tanya chose not to come to Gainesville because she wanted to stay home with her parents and because it was less expensive. But she probably would have stayed home without a financial motivation.

As she put it, quote, "There are some students who want the college life, but there are also some students like me who are more introverted."

Let me introduce you to one final UF online student, Stephanie Oweka.

Stephanie had always dreamed of going to the state university in her home state of California, and she was thrilled when she was admitted to UC–San Diego. But she works full time. UC-SD is purely residential, with daytime classes that would force her to quit her 9–6 job.

When Stephanie, who is 23, added the cost of not working to paying UC-SD's tuition, she found it was better to pursue her degree online.

That's how she became the first out-of-state student in the UF microbiology program.

There are many more students in Florida like Christy, Andrew, and Tanya. There are also many more students nationally like Stephanie. In the best tradition of our commitment to access, if these students have achieved the high standards required to enter UF, they deserve that opportunity—even if we can't squeeze one more undergraduate onto our Gainesville campus.

We are inventing the future by drawing on the strengths of our traditions—in this case, access, which has been a UF core principle since its inception.

That brings me to how we will use the E-Campus to renew our traditional focus on teaching and the legacy of academic excellence.

Let's start with some basics. Students admitted to the E-Campus must have the same high grades and test scores as those admitted to our regular campus. We do not foresee this as an impediment: in my estimation, half of the students who apply to current programs could be admitted—and would be successful—if we only had space for them on campus.

Just as our E-Campus students will be as excellent as our regular students, so it is with our E-Campus faculty.

All E-Campus classes will be taught by regular faculty, not a separate group of online faculty, as occurs at other universities.

Many faculty have legitimate concerns about maintaining instructional quality, building personal connections with students online, and assessing online student performance.

While the research on online outcomes is generally positive, we will be highly sensitive to these issues as we build the E-Campus.

We understand that the transition to an online class requires a huge investment of time and energy from faculty—and we will make a parallel investment in financial support, logistics, and guidance from the university. We have the resources in hand: the state provided UF $10 million to pay for upfront costs for the E-Campus, with $5 million annually in support costs.

That said, this new initiative is about much more than practicalities. Done right, online teaching completely reimagines that old standby, the 50-minute lecture. It challenges faculty to try bold new approaches—while challenging the university to bolster their experimentation and initiative.

This reevaluation benefits traditional students as well as those online. So say UF faculty who have tried online teaching.

Jennifer Clark is a UF senior lecturer in food and resource economics who has been teaching online classes for some time and taught one of our first Massive Open Online Classes, or MOOCs, this past year.

She says her transition to online required, quote, "a radical departure." But as she's become more expert, her work has helped her become more organized, a better communicator, and an enthusiast of new ways of delivering instruction.

As she herself says, she's a better teacher. And as more faculty follow in her footsteps, so UF will be a better teaching university. Again, inventing the future based on the strengths of our traditions—in this case, academic excellence.

This is also the idea behind the core curriculum for undergraduates.

Many of you are aware that it's been some time since we've thought about undergraduate education in terms of creating a shared experience that is unique to students at the University of Florida.

The legislature opened a door, giving us permission to require 12 hours of UF-only core courses. We begin this expansion by asking, "What is the purpose of undergraduate education?"

I'm only too aware of the political pressures to make universities even more utilitarian than we are. And given the economic difficulties, I agree that we need to prepare students for careers.

But isn't there also value in the concept of "What Is the Good Life?"—that we should help students question themselves and how they want to live? And shouldn't we also get students to think more deeply about technology's influence on their worldview? How about the concepts of community in a globalized world, or resiliency in the face of failure, or what the word "leadership" truly means?

These are the kinds of questions, rooted in our history of a strong liberal education, that I hope the UF core curriculum will address.

UF's deans got the ball rolling in August with a joint proposal for two new courses, "Design for Life" and "A Sustainable Life." It's a start, and we will devote the coming year to discussions with faculty on the quote "Florida Core."

Whatever curriculum we develop, this effort will join the E-Campus in forcing UF to put the spotlight back on undergraduate education. The "Florida Core" will also sew together myriad faculty, disciplines, and points of knowledge to elevate the undergraduate experience.

Once more, inventing the future by drawing on the strengths of our past.

That gets me to our drive to advance among the top public universities.

I'm aware that UF has sought to be considered among the nation's best universities for ... oh ... 100 years or so. I also know we've had to go it alone. Not only with fewer resources than many peers, but also without the state behind us.

This tradition ended with the legislature's acknowledgment of UF as Florida's leading research university—and its financial commitment toward us reaching the next level.

Only time will tell the impact of this alignment of the state and this university. But we will do our utmost to see that it is transformational—not only for us, but for all those whose lives are touched by our research and scholarship.

Tallahassee will give UF $15 million annually for the next five years. We will match this amount with donor funds. The UF Foundation will provide support with an $800 million capital campaign.

Right now, when we compare UF to the top 16 AAU public universities, it's clear that our biggest gaps relate to faculty numbers and prestige.

We are dead last in student-to-faculty ratio; dead last in number of National Academy members; 13th in faculty resources; 11th in faculty awards.

We need to improve in these standings. So, we will spend the bulk of our money on new faculty hires—including more than 100 new endowed professorships to be created by the UF Foundation's campaign.

We want new hires throughout the university, but we will invest strategically in departments or groups that have the most potential for national prominence. We will help good groups reach the tipping point to excellence, and will create new ones in areas of high demand.

As the E-Campus and the core curriculum will enhance UF's tradition of academic excellence, so this investment elevates UF in research.

It comes at an excellent time. Despite the myriad economic challenges, contracts and grants for the just-ended fiscal year are stable—falling about half a percentage point, from $644.3 million to $640.6 million.

We need more faculty, and more prominent faculty, to continue our performance in research funding . . . and research findings! More than anything else, the faculty represents the strength of the past that will help us invent the future.

As I wrap up, let me note that when UF was admitted to the AAU twenty-eight years ago, it was a recognition we were as good as the top sixty-two universities.

This year's designation as the state's highest-performing university is different. It's a challenge, a call to action.

It's saying, "We grant that you're our best university. We've heard your need for more resources. Now, prove to us that you can be a great university."

I hope you'll join me in answering that call.

Let's embrace the E-Campus as a return to a focus on teaching and academic excellence—and a new opportunity for national leadership in online education.

Let's use the core curriculum to create a rich and wonderful "Florida Core" undergraduate experience in the best tradition of liberal education at UF.

And amid stiffening competition for fewer research resources, let's get behind expanding research faculty and capabilities to vault UF to the nation's best.

Toward the end of his life, Robert Frost was asked whether he had hope for the future. "Yes," he replied. "And even for the past."

Likewise, I have great hope for our future because we are inventing it according to the best strengths and highest missions of our past.

BERNIE MACHEN has served as the eleventh president of the University of Florida since 2004. Prior to UF, he spent six years as president of the University of Utah. He also served as provost and executive vice president for academic affairs at the University of Michigan and dean of the University of Michigan School of Dentistry. He is a past president of the American Association of Dental Schools and was a member of the Board of Trustees of the Salt Lake Olympic Organizing Committee.

AARON HOOVER is an award-winning speechwriter who has worked closely with President Machen since 2005. A former science writer and newspaper reporter, he is the executive speechwriter in the UF President's Office.

The University Press of Florida is the scholarly publishing agency for the State University System of Florida, comprising Florida A&M University, Florida Atlantic University, Florida Gulf Coast University, Florida International University, Florida State University, New College of Florida, University of Central Florida, University of Florida, University of North Florida, University of South Florida, and University of West Florida.